Memory Improvement

Techniques to Reach New Heights in Life, Training Your Brain to Reach Your Full Potential and Achieve Success, Boosting Memory for Adults Students

Written By: Panagiotis Papadopoulos

© Copyright 2020 - All rights reserved.

Contents

You'll also be able to:

- Recite the order of a deck of cards as they were played
- Calculate the day of the week for any date from the year 1800 to 2099
- Recognize the names and faces of people you've just met
- Adopt the proper reading, writing, and reviewing techniques to ace your courses
- Expand your vocabulary and decipher the meanings of new words
- Remember where you left your car keys

We'll start off in Chapter 1 by discussing what memory is. This book will focus primarily on the scientific view of memory, as explored by cognitive scientists, psychologists, physicians, and educators. Yet, we'll also take a look at the cultural perspectives offered by social historians and the spiritual perspectives offered by different religions. We'll briefly overview the different hemispheres, lobes, limbic tissues, and neurons in the brain, learning how they contribute to your overall memory. We'll discuss the three-part process of how memories are encoded, stored, and retrieved, including the types of long-term memories our brains form through association. We'll finish the chapter by examining some of the factors that contribute to everyday forgetfulness, along with more serious forms of memory loss, like dementia.

Chapter 2 is where we'll dig deeper into the relationship between memory and learning. We'll discuss different theories and methods for measuring intelligence, from Sperry's Split Brain Theory, to Binet's IQ test, to Gardner's Theory of Multiple Intelligences. Having a solid understanding of what intelligence is and which learning methods you favor will help you choose the correct brain training techniques to help you improve your memory.

In Chapter 3, we'll begin to talk about mnemonics, which are different memory techniques you can use to remember information. We'll learn how ancient societies used mnemonics throughout their everyday lives, then discuss some popular mnemonic devices that form the basis of memory training. These include simple word associations, acronyms, acrostics, rhymes, and songs. We'll continue this discussion in Chapters 4 and 5 by looking at complex and multi-purpose mnemonic systems. We'll review the three main systems outlined by Tony Buzan, along with some Link System and Peg System methods favored by eight-time world memory champion Dominic O'Brien.

There are also several mnemonic techniques that you can adopt for specific tasks, like calculating dates from the last two centuries, organizing information into a mind map, or remembering names and faces in a crowd of strangers. We'll discuss these specialized methods in further detail in Chapter 6.

In Chapter 7, we'll learn some additional tips and tricks to boost your memory, even when you're not explicitly brain training. These range from expanding your everyday vocabulary to learning proper reading and reviewing techniques. We'll also discover some fun, memory-friendly hobbies you can try out in your spare time. These include logic-based pursuits, like solving puzzles and creating maps, along with more creative-based pursuits, like drawing, painting, and dream journaling.

Chapter 8 is where we'll discuss some healthy habits to improve your memory, such as maintaining a good posture, exposing yourself to fresh outdoor air, eating food rich in omega-3s and antioxidants, reducing your alcohol and marijuana consumption, exercising regularly, and getting the right amount of sleep every night.

Finally, in Chapter 9, we'll review some additional things to keep in mind while completing your brain training. By believing in the power of your brain, taking frequent breaks, and learning from your mistakes, you'll gain the confidence to continue with your brain training whenever you're feeling discouraged or considering giving up.

No brain is perfect. Yet, whether you're 18 or 80, you can improve your memory as long as you're dedicated to doing so. Even after a couple weeks of brain training, you'll be amazed by the capabilities you never knew you had. After a few years, you may even become the next world memory champion! Or at least the only one in your family with a fine-tuned Memory Palace.

First things first, let's get started on the basics of memory training. O'Brien (2016) suggests finding a seat in a comfortable room free from visual and auditory distractions. If you don't like working in silence, you can always play some mid-tempo classical music to help you focus (you can even find specific brain training playlists on YouTube and Spotify). You may also wish to make yourself enough room to get up and move around whenever you need to take a break, perhaps to do a bit of stretching or light jogging.

Once you've found your space, sit up straight, cue up the Mozart, give your fingertips a nice big stretch, and get ready to unlock your true memory potential.

CHAPTER - 01

Memory 101 – What It Is, How It Works

Memory is one of those abstract concepts that we hardly ever take the time to think about. Yet, it's such an important feature of everyday life! It's the foundation of learning and an essential component of our cultural and individual identities. It's a complex mental process that engages many different areas of our brains as we encode, store, and retrieve short- and long-term information. And when it goes wrong, it can have disastrous effects on our physical and emotional health.

This chapter will give you a quick overview of what memory is and how it works. This way, you'll have the proper background to begin your brain training exercises, having a solid understanding of how and why they benefit your long-term memory.

What Is Memory?

There are three major perspectives about memory. Each one contributes to our overall understanding of this complex phenomenon. This book will focus mainly on the scientific view of memory. Still, it's important to keep in mind that memory can mean something entirely different for different people, from the veteran neuroscientist explaining his new discovery to the young jingle dress dancer participating in her first powwow (Figure 2).

Figure 2: Indigenous people often have strong connections to the cultural view of memory, which allows them to pass on knowledge and traditions (G, 2015).

Scientific View

Merriam-Webster defines memory as "the store of things learned and retained from an organism's activity or experience" (Memory, n.d.). This is the classic scientific definition, based on the biological processes in our brains that process, store, and retrieve information.

According to this view, memory is the foundation of all learning (Harrison & Hobbs, 2010). Without it, we would never be able to recall facts, figures, or formulas and apply them to new problems. More importantly, we would never be able to accomplish even the simplest everyday tasks like speaking a language, climbing the stairs, or avoiding a hot burner with our bare hands.

Cognitive scientists, neuroscientists, physicians, psychologists, linguists, and educators are just some of the many professionals who study memory scientifically. Their methods include behavioral experiments, computer simulations, and brain imaging. The two most popular types of brain imaging are fMRI *(functional magnetic resonance imaging)* scans, which measure oxygenated blood flow in different areas of the brain, and EEGs *(electroencephalograms)*, which measure electric signals from *neurons* (brain cells).

Still, not everyone is satisfied with this purely scientific view of memory. Many cultural historians, anthropologists, sociologists, and even archaeologists have argued for a broader understanding that recognizes the role of memory in human society as a whole.

Cultural View

We often think of memory as being an individual experience. Yet, as many social scientists point out, *cultural memory* is just as powerful as personal memory. These collective memories, which are shared by a group of people, play an important role in passing on traditions, commemorating historical events, and shaping community identities (Assmann, 2008). Unlike personal memory, cultural memory can transcend individual life spans, lasting for dozens or even hundreds of generations. It is responsible for creating the present from the past, either actively through monuments, festivals, and oral histories, or else passively through libraries and archives.

French social historians of the Annales school were the first to become interested in the cultural view of memory (Confino, 2008). Scarred by the global chaos of World War I, they argued that memory is the best way to understand history, not as a biography of political or religious leaders, but as a shared system of beliefs and emotions about the past. By the 1990s, memory studies took the social sciences by storm and continues to play a big part in disciplines like cultural studies.

Still, both the scientific and cultural views of memory fail to recognize many of the features non-academics associate with memory, especially as they relate to emotions, souls, and spirits. We'll discuss this personal/spiritual view in the following section.

Personal/Spiritual View

For many people, memory is much more than a system of information or a vehicle for traditions. According to Harrison & Hobbs (2010), our memories are strongly connected to our emotions and experiences. We associate different events from our past with feelings of happiness, sadness, anger, disgust, or fear. These feelings make an imprint in our minds and shape the way we make decisions. Many also associate memories with people they care about, cherishing physical and mental reminders of family vacations, outings with friends, or even simple dinner conversations with their partners. In short, our memories are key factors in defining who we are as people.

Many religions, like Christianity, see memory as a part of an individual's soul (Buzan, 2006). Others, like Buddhism, reject the idea of an individual soul, but consider memory as an important vehicle for compassion toward others (Begley, 2008). Both Christian and Buddhist scholars believe that the human mind in general has a dual identity, partly physical and partly non-physical.

It's much more difficult to study the potential non-physical aspects of memory, especially since we don't even understand everything about the physical aspects. Nonetheless, the past few decades of research has helped us refine the scientific view. And the more we learn, the more we realize that memory cannot be reduced to a simple storage system of information.

How Does Memory Work?

Many people compare memory to a computer hard drive or a filing cabinet, but the reality is much more complicated than that. Memory is not a physical entity that can be pinpointed to a specific location in the brain. Instead, it's more like an experience, helping us to make sense of the past, present, and future through an enormous series of synaptic connections.

Before we learn about how memories are made and retrieved, let's look at the organ that makes it all possible: your brain.

Meet Your Brain

It's hard to believe that 95% of our current knowledge about the human brain has only been discovered in the last 30 years (Amen, 2017; Buzan & Harrison, 2010; Harrison & Hobbs, 2010). And with new advancements in imaging technology, neuroscientists are learning more and more everyday. This is what we know so far about the lump of folded, gray matter that allows our memories to exist (Figure 3).

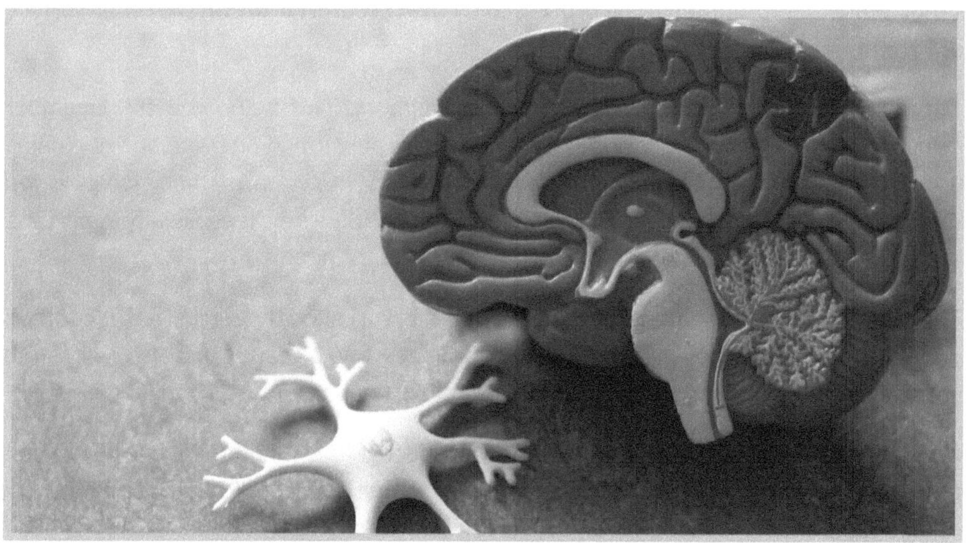

Figure 3: Model of the brain showing the limbic system, plus a neuron (Weermeijer, 2019).

Human brains are split down the center by a ridge of nerve fibers called the *corpus callosum*. This divides your brain into a *right* and *left hemisphere*. Each hemisphere contains one half of four different lobes. At the front of your brain is the *frontal lobe*. This lobe, which is more developed in humans than any other species, is associated with focus, problem solving, and controlling impulses. Beneath the frontal lobe is the *temporal lobe*, which controls sound, speech, and emotion. Above this is the parietal lobe, which is linked to spatial awareness and sensations like touch, pain, and body temperature. At the very back of the brain is the *occipital lobe*, which processes visual information.

All four of these lobes are associated with certain aspects of memory. Covering the front of the frontal lobe is the *prefrontal cortex*. This is the "executive center" of the brain. It's responsible for complex cognitive functions, like storing short-term memory and recalling long-term memory.

The temporal lobe is the site of the *limbic system*, which controls your basic emotions, instincts, and drives. The most important limbic structures are the *hippocampi*. The hippocampus in each hemisphere of your brain is responsible for converting short-term memories into long-term memories, processing spatial layouts, and connecting names and information to different objects. In front of each hippocampus is an *amygdala*. Amygdalae create emotional responses, which help you to remember painful situations in order to avoid them and pleasurable situations in order to repeat them. Finally, the *hypothalamus* relays nerve signals to and from the rest of your body, while the *thalamus* sends sensory information to be processed by the cerebral cortex on the outer surface of your brain.

The parietal lobe is associated with spatial memory. This helps you to remember directions and to perform actions like writing with a pencil, adding sums, and buttoning up a dress shirt. Finally, the occipital lobe is associated with visual memory. It allows you to recognize lights, shapes, colors, and shades. The occipital lobe is especially important, as our visual senses account for 75% of our overall learning.

There is also a limbic structure at the base of the brain called the *cerebellum*. It controls your basic survival functions, like breathing, balance, and digestion. It's also associated with muscle memory and plays an important role in helping you learn languages.

With so many areas of our brains serving different cognitive functions, it can be difficult to imagine how it all fits together. Our brains accomplish this task thanks to a network of 86 billion neurons. These cells relay information from inside and outside your body to the central nervous system, up your spine, and into your brain, which processes the information and creates a response. Neurons are connected to each other by receivers called *dendrites* and send electrical signals through transmitters called *axons*, which are protected by a layer of tissue called the *myelin sheath*. In between dendrites and axons are gaps called *synapses*. Each synapse connects about 1000 neurons, which comes out to over 100 trillion synaptic connections in your brain alone.

Experts are still unsure exactly how our brains store memories at cell level. Yet, some studies suggest that RNA plays a role *(ribonucleic acid)* (Buzan, 2006). RNA are single strands of DNA *(deoxyribonucleic acid)* that carry information about how to make proteins for our vital bodily functions. Experiments on lab rats imply that their RNA production changes when they learn new information. When one rat receives an RNA transplant from another rat, the first rat can perform tasks that only the second rat had been taught. Still, we need further research on human RNA production before we jump to any conclusions.

Perhaps the most important discovery of the past few decades has been the concept of *neuroplasticity* (Begley, 2008). This means that our brain structure is always changing. Neurons are constantly forming new connections with each other, allowing us to learn new information throughout our lives. Furthermore, while scientists originally believed that our brains never create new neurons, they now recognize that *neurogenesis* occurs right up until we turn 80! This just goes to show how limitless our memories are, provided that our brains are performing as they should.

The Three Stages of Healthy Memory

With such a complicated system of neurons, limbic structures, and lobes, it's impossible to calculate how much information the average human brain can hold. What is clear, however, is that our brains have a tried and true system for creating memories.

According to researchers at Harvard University, memory consists of two distinct but interdependent processes (Derek Bok Center, 2011). The first is an *unconscious process*, which includes functions like recalling information or performing everyday routines. This process is prone to errors, because it's based on quick, automatic reflexes. The second is a *conscious process*, which includes analysing information and solving problems. This process is more reliable, because it depends on slow, careful decision making. Still, as our minds become comfortable with conscious memory tasks, they soon become unconscious and instinctual. This allows us to multitask and invest our energy into learning new information.

When your memory is working as it should be, there are three stages in the remembering process (Derek Bok Center, 2011; Harrison & Hobbs, 2010). The first stage is *encoding*. Within one-to-two seconds, your brain processes *visual, acoustic* (sound-based), *semantic* (meaning-based), or *tactile* (sensation-based) information and decides whether or not it is meaningful. If it is, this *sensory memory* will be kept. Otherwise, it will be discarded.

It's important for your brain to filter out most of this sensory information in order to maintain focus and keep from overloading. This happens unconsciously, but you can also contribute to the process by deliberately not paying attention to your surroundings.

The second stage is *storage*. Your brain first stores new items of information as a 15-30 second *short-term memory*. Brains can only store five to nine of these memories at a single time. If we want to add a tenth item, we must forget one of the others. This is an evolutionary adaptation that helps us focus on important tasks by forgetting information that is not permanently relevant to us, like a temporary pin number for resetting a password. Most acoustic and visual memories tend to be short-term, unless we hear or see them repeatedly.

If your brain decides that the memory is important enough to remember for more than 30 seconds, the hippocampus will transform it into a *working memory* lasting 60 seconds to an hour, and eventually into a *long-term memory* that will last for the rest of your life. Long-term memories are stored in different areas of your brain, depending on the type of memory.

The final stage in the memory process is *retrieval*. We never remember information exactly as it was stored. Instead, we recreate it from scratch by stimulating nerve pathways. This is why our memories can change over time. Short-term memories are usually remembered as sequential lists. Yet, we tend to convert them into long-term memories when we associate them with other information, especially based on our emotions or personal experiences. We'll discuss the power of association in greater detail in Chapter 3.

According to Amen (2017), there are six types of long-term memories. These include:

Explicit memories: consciously-formed information. They can be *declarative* (related to knowledge), *episodic* (related to events and experiences), *semantic* (related to the meanings of words and ideas), or *flashbulb* (related to emotional situations).

Implicit memories: unconsciously-formed information. The two main types are *muscle memory*, which includes automatic movements like riding a bike or playing an instrument, and *emotional memory*, which includes unconscious reactions to happy, sad, or fearful situations.

Verbal memories: words and other features of language, like hand gestures.

Spatial memories: information for navigating environments and spaces.

Visual memories: perceptions of the world and mental images.

Associative memories: connections between naturally unrelated items, like hearing a bell ring and expecting someone at your front door.

We often associate having a good memory with having a *photographic* or *eidetic memory* (Harrison & Hobbs, 2010). This is a type of visual memory that occurs when you perfectly remember the arrangement of items you have seen. Photographic memories tend to be short-term, with good reason. When people convert them into long-term memories, their concentration skills tend to suffer. This is because the new information they learn creates an uncontrollable and distracting series of associations in their minds.

Yet, unfortunately, even our long-term memory process can be prone to errors, as we'll see in the following section.

Forgetting and Memory Loss

As cultural historian Aleida Assmann notes, memory is "a perpetual interaction between remembering and forgetting" (2008, p. 97). Despite our unlimited memory potential, there are instances when we fail to remember important things, like a family member's birthday or the answer to a quiz question.

Forgetfulness is especially concerning for older adults (Figure 4). Nyberg et al. (2003) blame older adults' weak working memories on reduced dorsal-frontal activity in the frontal lobe and shrinkage of the prefrontal cortex. The younger adults in their study could recall on average an additional 5.12 words in mnemonic systems tests than the older adults, who recalled 3.75 words on average. Yet, they also acknowledge that older adults are more stubborn about learning new memory techniques. This could be a greater source of their poor performance than their brain structures.Other studies show that even 80- and 90-year-olds can have the same memory power as 20- and 30-year-olds, provided they regularly practice and engage with mentally stimulating activities (Begley, 2008; Harrison & Hobbs, 2010).

Among younger adults especially, the most common cause for forgetfulness is stress. When you feel stressed, your brain becomes inefficient by releasing excessive amounts of cortisol, which blocks new neurons from forming in your hippocampus. This is especially disastrous for spatial memory, where people often forget where they put their keys or which way they turn to walk to the appropriate bus stop.

Another common factor is lack of interest. When you do not concentrate on the information you are learning, you are more likely to forget it. Engaging in mindful activities and developing fun ways to learn new information is one way to help you remember better. We'll discuss these activities in further detail in Chapter 7.

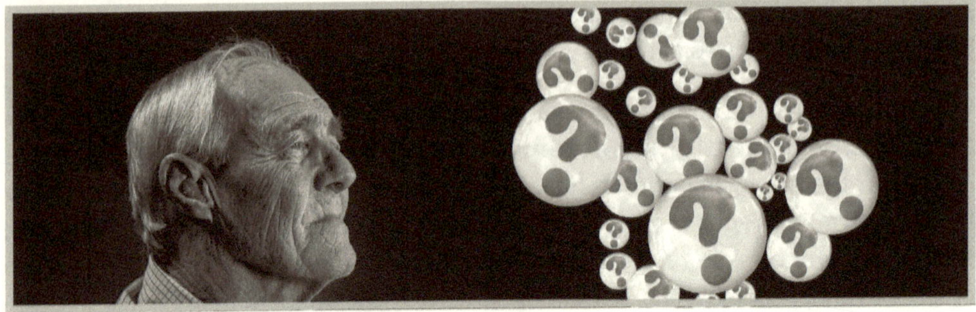

Figure 4: Older adults often blame their poor memories on "senior moments" (Altmann, 2017).

Nonetheless, dementia-related memory loss is still a concern for older adults, with over 36 million people across the world suffering from Alzheimer's, the most common dementia disorder (Chancellor, et al., 2014). Symptoms include not only memory loss, but also depression, apathy, aggression, hallucinations, and sleep deprivation. With no cure on the horizon, the number of incidents are expected to near 100 million in the next 30 years.

According to Dr. Daniel Amen, there are 11 main risk factors associated with dementia (2017, "The Program"). They can be remembered by the acronym BRIGHT MINDS (we'll discuss acronyms and other mnemonic devices in further detail in Chapter 3). These letters stand for:

Blood Flow: Blood flow to the brain is decreased by conditions like high blood pressure, heart disease, atherosclerosis, and stroke.

Retirement/Aging: People over 50 who do not engage in new learning activities risk lower memory performance.

Inflammation: High homocysteine amino acid levels, high C-reactive protein (CRP) levels, and low omega-3 levels are symptoms of inflammation, which decreases blood flow to non-injured areas (including the brain).

Genetics: Dementia disorders, like Alzheimer's, are inherited through the e4 APOE gene.

Head Trauma: Concussions and other forms of head trauma increase your risk of memory loss by directly impacting the performance of your brain.

Toxins: Exposure to drugs and alcohol, environmental pollution, chemotherapy, and other toxins may interfere with your memory.

Mental Health: Stress, anxiety, depression, bipolar disorder, attention deficit hyperactivity disorder (ADHD), post-traumatic stress disorder (PTSD), and schizophrenia all interfere with your neurochemistry and increase your risk for memory loss.

Immunity/Infection Issues: Low Vitamin D levels, autoimmune disorders like arthritis and multiple sclerosis (MS), chronic fatigue syndrome, and untreated infections like Lyme disease, syphilis, or herpes can all contribute to memory problems.

Neurohormone Deficiencies: Low thyroid hormone levels (hypothyroidism), high cortisol levels, estrogen/progesterone levels in women, and testosterone levels in men and women create high risks for memory loss.

Diabesity: Diabetes and obesity both put you at risk for high blood sugar, which prevents your neurons from receiving nutrients.

Sleep Issues: Chronic insomnia and sleep apnea (obstructed airways during sleep) prevents your brain from recharging and undergoing neurogenesis.

Addressing all of these factors can help reduce your risk for dementia disorders. We'll discuss some of these brain health-friendly habits in Chapter 8.

While we may scold ourselves for being forgetful, it's important to remember that some forgetting of information is a natural part of the memory process (Wimber, et al., 2015). Scientists call this "adaptive forgetting," because it helps us focus on the most important information and discard unpleasant memories that interfere with our mental health.

Yet, most scientists agree that the information we learn is always stored in our brains, even if we can't recall it. This is good news, meaning that we can always find new ways to recover this information and grow our intelligence as a result.

CHAPTER - 02

Getting Started

As we discussed in Chapter 1, memory and learning are interchangeable processes. When you make a conscious effort to improve your memory, your brain as a whole will work much more quickly and efficiently.

Before we dive into some tips and tricks to boost your memory, let's take a quick look at what it means to be intelligent and how you can use your intelligence to create your own brain training program. Becoming aware of the strengths and weaknesses of your brain will help you discover your preferred learning methods. This, in turn, will help you decide which memory-training techniques are the best options for you.

Understanding Intelligence

What comes to mind when you hear the word intelligent (Figure 5)? Do you think of rocket scientists, college professors, and Nobel Prize winners? Do you picture computers with complex binary code? Blackboards full of trigonometric figures? Test tube racks filled with brightly colored fluids? For many people, these are the types of images that come to mind.

Figure 5: A common view of intelligence, complete with a chalkboard, light bulb, and hard-working student (Adrian, 2018).

Yet, as Harrison & Hobbs (2010) argue, intelligence is a lot more complicated than this. Broadly speaking, it means:

- Being perceptive about your surroundings
- Taking careful note of the individual people, places, objects, and activities you encounter
- Thinking critically and creatively in the classroom, at the office, at home, and everywhere in between
- Easily understanding new concepts
- Applying your knowledge to solve new problems and adapt to new situations

To understand this complicated nature of intelligence, memory experts used to classify people as being right-brain dominant, left-brain dominant, or both-brain dominant. They also measured intelligence through IQ (intelligence quotient) tests. Since the late 1980s, we've realized that there are many different types of intelligence that cannot be pinpointed to a specific hemisphere of the brain or measured by a single test. Before we explore these newer findings, let's take a look at the more traditional theories.

Left-Brain vs. Right-Brain Dominance

Many of our popular ideas about intelligence come from split-brain research (Buzan, 2006; Buzan & Harrison, 2010). This was pioneered in the late 1950s by neuropsychologist Roger Sperry. He noticed that the brain is divided into two hemispheres and assigned specific skills and personality traits to each hemisphere. The left hemisphere, also called the *left brain*, is associated with logic, critical reasoning, language, and number skills. The right hemisphere, or *right brain*, is associated with creativity, intuition, spatial awareness, and artistic and musical skills. Sperry also argued that brain dominance has an inverse relationship with hand dominance. This means that left-brained individuals favor their right hand, while right-brained individuals favor their left.

Experts who support split-brain theory argue that most people tend to be either left- or right-brain dominant. Yet, your overall knowledge improves when you participate in two different activities that correspond to opposite sides of your brain. For example, if you study computer coding on Tuesday nights and watercolor painting on Thursday nights, both your coding and painting skills will improve much quicker than if you decided to only learn one or the other.

Other people may be both-brain dominant. Indeed, many of the smartest humans in history developed skills associated with different sides of their brain. This includes medieval astronomer/poet Omar Khayyám, Renaissance inventor/artist Leonardo da Vinci, and 20th-century physicist/violinist Albert Einstein. So, instead of accepting that you can only be a JavaScript coder or a landscape painter, why not challenge yourself to do both? Who knows? You might even go down in history as the next Einstein.

That being said, most modern researchers have challenged split-brain theory (Harrison & Hobbs, 2010; Nielsen et al., 2013). Although language areas tend to be located on the left-side of the brain, while visual areas tend to be located on the right, there is no evidence that we only ever use one hemisphere at one time. Certain tasks may rely on more "left-brain" or "right-brain" functions. Yet, most humans show at least some degree of lateral, or both-sided, activity, whether they're entering code, adding brushstrokes, or even learning mnemonics. The more areas of the brain we engage with, the more neural connections we form. This makes it more difficult to make a clear-cut distinction between left- and right-brain dominance.

Still, as we'll learn throughout this book, participating in activities that engage many different areas of your brain is a surefire way t0 boost your overall intelligence and improve your memory in the process.

What is IQ?

The *IQ test* is a technique for measuring intelligence, developed in 1905 by French psychologist Alfred Binet (Gardner & Hatch, 1989; Harrison & Hobbs, 2010). It's a problem-solving test that assesses three types of knowledge: verbal, numerical, and visual-spatial. IQ tests often ask you to define common words, solve simple math problems, and identify shapes and pictures. Results are scored out of 100 and compared to the statistical norm for other people your age.

The main problem with the standard IQ test is that it is only based on three kinds of intelligence. Even then, the visual-spatial component of the test often takes a backseat to the verbal and numerical components. This is problematic, because 40% of our brains are involved in seeing and processing visual information. Furthermore, we now know that different areas of the brain are associated with different forms of knowledge. Therefore, damage to one area might affect someone's verbal skills but not their numerical skills, or vice versa. In this case, a person might fail the verbal section of the IQ test and score above-average on the numerical section. Does this make them unintelligent? Or are they intelligent in a different way than other participants? The IQ test doesn't offer a clear-cut answer for this problem.

Finally, having a high IQ doesn't necessarily mean that you have a strong memory. In an extreme case, a person could cram their working memory right before the test, then forget everything an hour later.

As we've discussed, long-term memory is closely linked to personal experiences and emotions, both of which are ignored by the IQ test. Therefore, someone could live through an emotionally-charged historical event, like a civil war. They could strongly remember all of the figures, ideologies, and battles associated with it. Yet, if they had trouble picking out shapes in an abstract painting or performing basic multiplication, they might be classified as having a low IQ.

Because of these many limitations, IQ tests remain controversial measures of intelligence. Instead, many researchers have turned to Gardner's Theory of Multiple Intelligences as a more accurate framework.

Theory of Multiple Intelligences

Psychologist Howard Gardner challenged the notion of a single intelligence by outlining seven different types. Gardner & Hatch (1989) define them as the following:

Logical-Mathematical Intelligence: identifying logical or numerical patterns, and developing long chains of reasoning.

Linguistic Intelligence: sensitivity to words and their sounds, rhythms, and meanings in a language or languages.

Musical Intelligence: appreciation of and talent for rhythm, pitch, timbre, and other forms of musical expression.

Spatial Intelligence: high perception of the visual-spatial world and skills to accurately transform it.

Bodily-Kinesthetic Intelligence: fine-tuned control for moving the body and handling objects.

Interpersonal Intelligence: identifying and appropriately responding to other people's feelings and desires.

Intrapersonal Intelligence: detailed knowledge of your own feelings and desires, and using this knowledge to guide your behavior.

The Theory of Multiple Intelligences overcomes the logical-mathematical and linguistic bias of IQ tests by broadening the definition of intelligence. For example, a car salesman could be just as intelligent as a rocket scientist. The only difference is that a car salesman has excellent interpersonal skills, while a rocket scientist has excellent logical-mathematical skills.

Additionally, just like Sperry's Split-Brain Theory, people can gravitate toward a single type of intelligence or use multiple types at the same time. Indeed, many career paths require a combination of intelligences. For example, a singer-songwriter would need a high degree of linguistic and musical intelligence, while a surgeon would need logical-mathematical and bodily-kinesthetic intelligence.

This theory also provides a reasonable way to test your overall smarts. By performing activities that rely on different intelligences, like choreographing an interpretive dance to a popular song or illustrating an algebra problem, you can identify where your weaknesses are and work on improving them.

Understanding which types of intelligence you favor can also help you decide how to improve your memory. If you lean toward spatial intelligence, incorporating visual arts into your memory training will be beneficial. Or, if you lean toward intrapersonal intelligence, you may wish to connect things you want to remember to your personal experiences. Experiment with different styles and see which ones work best for your strengths.

Understanding Brain Training

Now that you're familiar with your own brain's strengths and weaknesses, it's time to put your intelligence to good use in a brain training program. By doing so, you'll be able to improve your memory in the best way possible, according to your individual tastes and goals (Figure 6).

What Is Brain Training?

According to Harrison & Hobbs (2010), *brain training* consists of activities designed to 'exercise' your brain. Just like your arms and legs, your brain needs to stay in shape in order to properly function. Brain training helps you do this by improving your working memory, your problem-solving skills, and your overall intelligence. It can also help you improve your focus and increase your speed of thinking, among other benefits.

There are many different types of brain training techniques. Some focus on specific skills. These include improving your mental math with multiplication problems or testing your visual recognition with "spot the difference" exercises. Others have more far-reaching effects, combining different skills to exercise multiple intelligences at the same time. Many brain training techniques are designed for visual learning, verbal learning, or both. Some also involve kinesthetic exercises to help link concepts to your muscle memory.

Figure 6: They say elephants never forget. And with the proper brain training techniques, neither will you (Buissine, 2016).

In this book, we'll focus specifically on brain training techniques that boost your memory skills. These include creating acronyms to remember phone numbers, using mind maps to plan speeches, and even learning how to remember names and faces at your next dinner party. That's not even the best part. Many of these techniques will also expand your vocabulary, improve your concentration, and develop your creative thinking.

Does It Actually Work?

It may seem like wishful thinking that inventing wacky sentences or doodling on a piece of paper can help you become less forgetful. Yet, studies show that practicing these techniques may do just that.

To assess the effects of brain training, a University of Michigan study had groups of students complete daily brain-training exercises for 8, 12, 17, or 19 days (cited in Harrison & Hobbs, 2010). They discovered that the longer students spent brain-training, the more they improved on general cognitive tests.

Similarly, in their 2003 study, Nyberg, et al. assessed the effects of learning mnemonic systems on the brains of younger and older adults. As we'll learn in Chapter 4, mnemonic systems consist of substituting an abstract word for a concrete word and then associating that word with a mental image. They discovered that activity in the parietal and left hippocampal regions increases when people successfully learn these systems. Because the parietal and hippocampal areas are associated with learning locations, associating images with locations, and connecting words to their meanings, Nyberg et al. concluded that mnemonic systems can benefit learners of any age.

Still, the only way to decide if brain training is right for you is to give it a try. Let's get started by diving into the basics of mnemonics.

CHAPTER - 03

Basic Mnemonics

Mnemonics are words, images, patterns and other learning techniques that are designed to help you remember things (Buzan & Harrison, 2010). They appeal to your imagination, your reasoning skills, and your five senses to connect words, images, and patterns to more complex ideas.

In this chapter, we'll cover a brief history of mnemonics, learning how they were used in ancient societies and how these early origins still shape our learning today. We'll also discover some of the most popular mnemonic devices, including visual and verbal associations, acronyms, acrostics, rhymes, and songs.

The Birth of Mnemonics

Before the invention of writing, humans had to remember important information by listening and repeating (Buzan, 2006; Harrison & Hobbs, 2010). Oral art forms, like storytelling, were important vehicles of knowledge, using repetitive wordplay and evocative imagery to share ideas and emotions. Even as societies became literate, they continued to rely on this interplay between the visual and verbal in order to preserve individual and collective memories.

Figure 7: The ancient Greeks worshipped Memory as an important goddess (Ranya, 2015).

The word mnemonics comes from Mnemosyne, the ancient Greek goddess of memory. It's easy to see why the ancient Greeks worshipped Memory (Figure 7). Poets called on her to help them remember the lines of Homer's epics while reciting them at cultural festivals. Politicians used her powers to remember long speeches to recite in the ecclesia (democratic assembly), so they could sway other citizens to vote in their favor while saving money on expensive paper. Plus, historians, musicians, actors, dancers, and astronomers hailed Mnemosyne as the mother of the nine Muses, the goddesses of the arts and sciences. This genealogy shows that the Greeks were ahead of their time in recognizing that memory is the foundation of all knowledge.

Modern western thinking owes a lot to the ancient Greeks. Memory studies is no exception. We no longer believe, as the ancients did, that memory stems from a balance of temperatures or air circulation in the body. Nor do we see our minds as a wax tablet, permanently etched on by our impressions of the world. Yet, experts still agree that long-term memory is based on two foundations: *imagination and association.*

To remember any piece of information, all you need to do is use your imagination to connect it with a known object, location, or concept. There are many ways to accomplish this, which you'll learn throughout this book. But for now, we'll focus on the basic mnemonic devices.

Popular Mnemonic Devices

Imagination and association come naturally together through mnemonic techniques that use visual and verbal cues to help us remember information (O'Brien, 2016). These techniques can be as complicated as developing an entire code to memorize number sequences. Or, they can be as simple as making connections between the sound of one word and the meaning of another.

In the rest of this chapter, we'll look at some simple but effective mnemonic devices that make great starting points on your memory training journey. You may even be familiar with some of these devices already.

To begin, we'll look at simple visual and verbal associations that connect new information to the way that words look and sound. We'll learn some abbreviations and extensions to help you reduce a complicated list of words or expand an unmemorable sequence of letters. We'll also branch into musical territory by analysing the effect of rhyme, rhythm, and tempo on your long-term memory.

Unless noted otherwise, all of the information in this section has been adopted from O'Brien (2016). The word definitions, here as well as elsewhere in this book, have been taken from Merriam-Webster.

Simple Word Associations

The most basic mnemonic device is the *simple word association*. This can be *visual*, based on what the word looks like, or *verbal*, based on what it sounds like.

Looking for letter patterns can be a useful visual tool to remember how to spell words correctly. The word separate has "a rat" inside. This will help you remember that the correct spelling is sep*arate* and not sep*erate*. Additionally, the word CEMETERY, in all caps, has three capital Es. By noting that these Es look like tombstones, you'll remember that the correct spelling is cEmEtEry and not cEmAtEry or cEmAtAry.

If you're a visual learner, you may also wish to draw out your associations to make them more memorable. You could draw two rats pulling apart the letters of "separate" and three E tombstones for CEMETERY. This technique can also work for memorizing words and their meanings. For example, yampee is another name for cush-cush, a type of yam that plays a big part in Latin American and Caribbean cuisines. To remember this, you could draw a yam with the letter P growing as a leaf out of the tuber. Whenever you come across the word in your Jamaican cookbook, you can associate it with your drawing and know instantly what it means.

Maybe you're not the best at drawing. Or maybe the words you need to remember don't lend themselves easily to visual associations. In this case, you may wish to use verbal associations instead. The most basic form of verbal association is the pun.

We often think of puns as being the hallmark of Dad jokes. Yet, they are one of the easiest mnemonic devices, exploiting words that sound like others to make them memorable. You may groan inwardly when you hear a joke like, "Why was the mushroom invited to the party? Because he was a *fungi*." But this wordplay around the homophones *fun guy* and *fungi* would be useful on a biology test, where you would need to remember the six Kingdoms of living things. Using this pun, it's easy to remember that mushrooms belong to Kingdom Fungi. You can even extend the pun to remember other Fungi members by saying that the mushroom "broke the *mold*," "has no *morels*," "is nothing but *truffle*," and "makes *20 mil, dude* (mildew)." Let your imagination run wild, and you'll be surprised how effectively a cringe-worthy pun can help you ace your test.

Jokes aside, simple puns are especially useful when trying to remember scientific terms or words borrowed from other languages. For example, if you are dissecting an earthworm in biology class and want to remember that earthworms belong to the *Annelid* phylum, you might name your worm something like "Anne," "Anna," or "Anneliese" as a pun on *Annelid*. Similarly, if you want to remember the meaning of the Yiddish-borrowed word *verklempt*, which means choked up with emotions, you might associate it as being "very clammed (up)." It may seem juvenile, but verbal puns form the basis of the expert-advocated LinkWord Technique, which we'll discuss in Chapter 5.

You can also use visual and verbal puns to remember the capitals of countries, by linking them to words or images that remind us of the countries. For example, to remember the Estonian capital Tallinn, you might draw two women named *Esther* and *Tonia* entering the *tall* door of an *inn*. For the Moroccan capital Rabat, you might picture a *rabbit* hopping through the airplane scene from Casablanca, or entering a bazaar. Here, sellers could offer colorful scarves, harissa peppers, couscous dishes, and any other item you might associate with Morocco.

In short, puns help you associate unknown words and concepts with familiar similar-sounding words and concepts. The danger with verbal word associations, however, is that it's easy to mistake the pun for the word itself. This can lead you to accidentally write *Rabbit* as the capital of Morocco during a pub quiz night or tell your friend that you're all "*verclammed*" after your latest breakup.

Use puns with caution and make sure you can correctly make the association between them and the words you're trying to learn.

Sometimes the information you want to remember doesn't lend itself easily to a simple visual or verbal association, especially when it's a list of words or a sequence of letters. This is where acronyms and acrostics, our next two mnemonic devices, come in handy.

Acronyms

Acronyms are a type of abbreviation, consisting of a single word that takes the first letter or first set of letters of other words. We see everyday acronyms most often as names of organizations, scientific techniques, and computer functions. These include WHO for the World Health Organization, RADAR for RAdio Detection And Ranging, and JPEG for Joint Photographic Experts Group.

Yet, acronyms can also help us remember items of information. For example, Amen (2017) uses BRIGHT MINDS as a mnemonic for dementia risk factors. You may be familiar with more popular acronyms, like HOMES for the five Great Lakes of North America (Huron, Ontario, Michigan, Erie, and Superior) or DR & MRS VANDERTRAMP for the French verbs that conjugate with *être* (to be) instead of *avoir* (to have) in the past tense. These include the verbs *Devenir* (to become), *Revenir* (to come back), *Monter* (to climb), *Rentrer* (to re-enter), *Sortir* (to exit), *Venir* (to come), *Aller* (to go), *Naître* (to be born), *Descendre* (to go down), *Entrer* (to enter), *Retourner* (to return), *Tomber* (to fall), *Rester* (to stay), *Arriver* (to arrive), *Mourir* (to die), and *Partir* (to leave).

Creating your own acronyms is a great way to remember short lists of objects, places, and concepts. The key is to pick memorable letter sequences that can be pronounced as a single word. This is what makes HOMES such a memorable acronym that wouldn't be possible with another arrangement, like MOHES or SHEOM.

Of course, the problem with acronyms is that sometimes they become so ingrained in your mind that you can't remember what they stand for. For example, the word HOMES is easy to remember, but what if you can't remember which lakes it includes? After all, there are many large lakes across Canada and the US that start with these five letters.

If you are unfamiliar with the Great Lakes area, you might easily mistake the O for Lake Okanagan or the S for Lake Sakakawea. Alternatively, you may remember the acronym HOMES, but not be able to recall what the letters stand for.

In this case, it might be easier to combine acronyms with visual associations. For example, you could imagine a series of five HOMES on an island in the middle of a great lake, with Canadian and American flags strung between them. To remember the five lakes that make up HOMES, you could fill each home with an occupant that reminds you of the lake's name, such as a *heron* for Lake Huron and an *eerie* ghost for Lake Erie. This might be more difficult for Ontario and Michigan, unless you've visited this province and state and can associate them with a specific person.

Still, if you're a verbal learner, you might find that acronyms are an easy mnemonic device to master and use throughout your daily life.

Acrostics

Acrostics, also called extended acronyms, are similar mnemonic devices to acronyms. They consist of short sentences, where the first letter of every word corresponds to a sequence of letters. These letters either stand on their own or form the first letters of a short list of words.

For example, the notes on the 6th to 1st strings on a guitar are EADGBE. On its own, this may be a difficult sequence to remember. Yet, many beginner guitarists learn the helpful acrostic "Eddie Ate Dynamite: Good-Bye Eddie" in order to identify this sequence. Similarly, before Pluto was demoted from its planet status, many elementary school students learned the order of planets from the sun as "My Very Eager Mother Just Served Us Nine Pizzas." This letter sequence corresponds to the order of Mercury, Venus, Earth, Mars, Jupiter, Saturn, Uranus, Neptune, and Pluto. To exclude Pluto from the acrostic, you might rewrite it as "My Very Eager Mother Just Served Us Nachos."

Acrostics can also be used to remember sequences of numbers. All you have to do is substitute each number for a word that contains that exact amount of letters. Let's say the PIN for your bank card is 5326. You can remember this by creating a short phrase where the first word has five letters, the second has three, the third has two, and the fourth has six. It might look something like this: Every (5) Day (3) Is (2) Payday (6).

Like acronyms, acrostics work best when you pick the catchiest, most memorable sentences that come to mind. It also helps when they're somehow associated with the sequence or list you're trying to remember. After all, the "Every Day Is Payday" acrostic reminds you that the number is associated with finance and not science or geography.

Although acrostics work like a charm for sequences of letters or numbers, it's more difficult when they substitute for other words in a short list. Like the HOMES acronym, the "My Very Eager Mother" acrostic may be easier to remember than the list of planets it stands for. This is also complicated by the fact that M appears twice in the acrostic, first as Mercury and then as Mars. It would be quite easy to make the mistake of writing the planet sequence as Mars, Venus, Earth, Mercury instead of Mercury, Venus, Earth, Mars.

Despite these difficulties, acrostics remain a popular way to remember useful information. Try it for yourself and see where it takes you.

Rhymes

Aside from puns, rhymes are one of the easiest verbal mnemonic devices. They make information easier to remember by creating rhythm and matching sounds. These sounds usually occur in the final syllables of lines as *end rhymes*. Yet, if you're feeling ambitious, you can also use *internal rhymes* in the middle of your lines.

Many end rhymes are already established mnemonics. For example, to remember the year that Christopher Columbus arrived in the Americas, many students recite "Back in 1492, Columbus sailed the ocean *blue*." In this instance, the word "blue," which is easily associated with the 'ocean,' helps you remember the year '1492.' Other rhymes are commonly used in everyday tasks, like converting tablespoons to teaspoons ("one big *T* equals teaspoons *three*") or forecasting rainy weather ("Red sky at *night*, sailors' *delight*; red sky in the *morning*, sailors take *warning*").

Again, rhymes are more effective when the topic relates to whatever information you need to remember. Yet, much like acronyms and acrostics, it's easy to get confused about some rhymes, especially when they involve longer numbers or long lists of information. For example, Columbus could have set sail in the year 1482, 1592, or any other four-digit year that rhymes with 'blue.'

Because of this, it may be more effective to combine rhymes with other mnemonic techniques. In Chapter 4, we'll learn about the Number-Rhyme Method, which uses a rhyming code to remember lists of up to ten items. Still, you can experiment on your own to see if simple rhyming works for you.

Songs

One mnemonic device that is often neglected by memory experts, but forms such a strong basis for early learning, is song. Though the links between song and memory are not conclusive, some studies suggest that remembering information through songs can improve your retention of information. Davis & Fan (2016) found that Chinese kindergarteners who were taught through song remembered English vocabulary, rhythm, grammar, and speech sounds better than those who were taught by *rote*, or repetitive, memorization.

Other studies show that even adults who aren't trained musicians have a strong memory for popular songs. In their 1996 study, Levitin & Cook discovered that 72% of their subjects were able to recall the tempos of popular songs like "Row, Row, Row Your Boat" and "We Wish You A Merry Christmas" within 8% of the actual tempo. One reason for this is that songs may act as 'earworms,' getting stuck in your head and making it easy for you to remember them (Davis & Fan, 2016). Pitch and tempo are usually processed in different areas in your brain, but memory for songs combines these two, strengthening your overall intelligence.

To maximize this 'earworm' potential, try reciting what you need to remember to the tune of a familiar song. You may find that giving this information rhythm and tempo makes it much easier to remember your boss's cell number, directions to your town's new Italian restaurant, or even the names of the bones in the human body. If you're a bodily-kinesthetic learner, you can even add choreography. See where this takes you!

Songs and other basic mnemonic devices are great when you want to remember small bits of information, like the year Columbus arrived in the Americas or the notes on your 6-string guitar. But what if you need to memorize a larger set of words or numbers, like a shopping list or the decimal values of pi? You could try to make up an acrostic based on your list or set the numbers to a catchy jingle. But you may find that the basic mnemonic devices just aren't cutting it.

This is where mnemonic systems come in, providing more robust techniques to help you improve your memory. We'll discuss the first set of these systems in Chapter 4.

Exercises

Think you've mastered the basic mnemonic devices? Test your knowledge by memorizing the following:

Proper spellings: accommodate, definitely, pronunciation

State capitals: Augusta (Maine), Topeka (Kansas), Salem (Oregon), Annapolis (Maryland)

Coordinating conjunctions: but, for, and, nor, or, so, yet

Continents of the world: Africa, Antarctica, Asia, Australia/Oceania, Europe, North America, South America

Fire safety technique: stop, drop, roll

CHAPTER - 04

Mnemonic Systems – Link and Peg

Mnemonic systems are multi-purpose tools that can help you remember almost any set of information by associating lists of words and numbers with mental images (Buzan, 2006). These images don't have to be photographic, but they should be vivid enough to make an impression. By filling your mind with colorful, rhythmic, dynamic, textured, and sensory images, you can create an absurd and imaginative, but orderly and memorable, collection of ideas.

In the following two chapters, we'll be discussing the three most popular mnemonic systems, along with the different methods associated with each. By familiarizing yourself with these systems, you'll be able to devise new ways to train your brain and broaden your memory potential.

Unless stated otherwise, the classifications in Chapters 4 and 5 have been adopted from Buzan (2006).

Link System

The *Link System* is the most basic mnemonic system. It helps you remember a short list by including each item in a vivid short story. To illustrate this system, let's say you need to buy six things:

- A travel mug
- A spatula
- Shoelaces
- Milk
- A phone charger
- Dog biscuits

Instead of writing it down or struggling to remember everything by heart, imagine yourself at your kitchen counter, filling your *travel mug*. You can feel the heat rising, wafting an irresistible dark-roast aroma. Once you have carefully screwed the lid of your mug, you turn to your stove and stir your freshly cracked eggs with a *spatula*. It scrapes against the frying pan with a grinding metallic sound that sets your teeth on edge. But your stomach growls in anticipation as the yolks and whites solidify.

Soon, your eggs are done. You use the spatula to scoop them onto your plate. Then, you head toward the fridge, but trip and lunge headfirst into the handle. Rubbing your head, you look down and realize your *shoelaces* are untied. You start on the left shoelace, bringing both ends together, looping one underneath the other, and pulling tightly. You make two bunny ears, loop one around the other, then pull once more. You repeat the process for the right shoelace.

Now that your shoelaces are properly tied, you open your refrigerator and reach for the *milk* carton. It crashes to the ground, soaking your shoes and seeping into your floorboards. You begin to wonder why you even bothered getting out of bed.

Your phone rings as you clean up. It's connected to the *phone charger* beside your fridge. Unplugging your phone, you are greeted by a "Where are you?" from your best friend. You were supposed to walk your dogs together this morning. Did you forget? Somewhat guiltily, you lie and tell them that you overslept, but you're on your way.

You hang up, scarf down your breakfast, grab your travel mug and call your beloved pooch, who is sleeping in her dog bed. She lazily opens one eye but does not come to you. You remind her that she loves the park. Still, she does not come. Sighing, you run back to the kitchen and grab your dog's favourite *biscuits*. It does the trick. She jumps up immediately, happily munching on the biscuit you give her. With your drink in one hand and your dog's leash in the other, you rush to the door as your phone rings again.

That's it. You can create whatever story you want to link those six items or any other items you need to remember. As long as you repeat your story a few times in your head and vividly imagine each section, you won't ever need a pen and paper.

The Link System doesn't just work with concrete words. You can also use it with a list of abstract words, as long as you associate each one with objects, people, animals, or locations. For example, to remember the most populated urban centres in Europe, memory champion Boris Nikolai Konrad recommends replacing the name of each city with two words that sound like the city or are somehow associated with it (TEDx Talks, 2016). You can substitute *moss* and *cow* for Moscow and *Pope* and *pizza* for Rome, and so on. Even when you cannot change the word, Konrad suggests creating action-driven mental images, like imagining *love* as two people kissing.

These concepts will also come in handy for the other mnemonic systems and methods in this book.

Journey Method

The main problem with the basic Link System is that there are no consistent connections between items. The Journey Method, also called the Method of Loci, improves on this by associating items with fixed points along a real or imagined journey (Harrison &

Hobbs, 2010; O'Brien, 2016). This journey can be any sort of sequence with definite loci, including the plot points of your favorite fantasy book or the sun salutation poses from your morning yoga routine. Eventually, you may want to imagine a real-life journey that is somehow connected to the information you need to remember, such as your route to your local gym for remembering sports statistics. But for now, imagine any journey of your choice, taking note of each landmark you pass (Figure 8).

Figure 8: To begin mapping your Journey Method, why not start in your own neighborhood? (Karabulut, 2019)

For example, you might begin at your *house*, pass underneath a *tree* on the sidewalk, cut through a park with a *play structure*, pass a *sandwich shop*, arrive at a plaza with a *fountain* and end your journey at a *bus shelter*. Once you've memorized each locus, you can start adding items associated with your shopping list.

To begin, imagine a doormat in front of your *house*, depicting a *coffee mug* with rising curls of steam. Someone has suspended a *spatula* on a branch of the *tree*, where it sways in the breeze. A little boy loses his *shoe* on the *play structure*. A *cow* stands in the doorway of the *sandwich shop* and moos. A businesswoman accidentally drops her *phone* into the *fountain* while passing by. Finally, you spot a *dog* with a *biscuit* in its mouth tied to a pole at the *bus shelter*.

The Journey Method is a favorite among memory champions, due in part to its flexibility. English memory champion Ben Pridmore used it to memorize a shuffled deck of cards in 26.28 seconds, while Malaysian memory champion Dr. Yip Swe Chooi used it to memorize an entire English-Chinese dictionary. Even if you're not interested in performing these extraordinary feats, you can still use it for everyday tasks, like remembering jokes, presentations, lines from a play, or directions to your doctor's new office.

Peg System

Unfortunately for Link System users, if you forget where you are at some point in your story or journey, you won't remember the rest of your items (Harrison & Hobbs, 2010). The basic *Peg System* improves on this by associating items with independent loci, like a series of pegs on a coat hanger. It helps when the loci you pick are familiar to you, like parts of your body, locations in your house, or a set series of images and words that substitute for numbers or letters.

This time, imagine each item on your shopping list attached to a part of your body. You begin by balancing a fragrant cappuccino in a *travel mug* on your *head*. Pretty impressive. But not as impressive as the spatula that you clench in your *mouth*. There's a *phone charger* draped across your *shoulders*, the transformer gently thumping against your chest as you steady your balance. In your *hands*, you hold a *milk* carton. Try not to drop it! In your pocket, you feel a bag of *dog biscuits* poking into your *stomach*. Worst of all, your *shoelaces* are tied together, restricting your *feet* as you press deeper into the ground to steady yourself.

For longer lists, you can include other body parts, like the eyes, nose, chest, and knees. Or, you could substitute your body for anything else with fixed 'pegs,' like a tree in your backyard or an analog clock face.

Sometimes you may need to remember items in a specific order. Sometimes you don't. The Peg System is flexible enough to accommodate both, with the Number-Shape, Number-Rhyme, Dominic, and Alphabet Methods adapted for sequential lists and the Memory Palace Method adapted for loosely organized lists.

Number-Shape Method

The *Number-Shape Method* helps you remember a list of items numbered one through ten by substituting each number with a shape it resembles. You might notice that the number 1 looks like a pencil. Or a pole. Or a lightsaber. The number 2 might look like a swan, the number 3 might look like lips, and so on. Let your imagination run wild and choose the shape that sticks out the most in your mind. These will become your *memory words*.

Once you have picked your memory words, try to imagine them as vividly as you can. What color is your lightsaber? Is your swan feathery or sleek? Are your lips covered in a sparkly gloss or are they dry and flaky? You can also draw your memory words to really commit them to memory.

Once you can successfully associate each number with a shape, you're ready to apply them to your shopping list. Let's say the rest of your numbers are a *sail* for number 4, a *pregnant woman* for number 5 and a *cherry* for number 6. You might stir your *travel mug* with a tiny *lightsaber*, listening to it cut through the sugar granules and feeling it warm your coffee. Your *swan* uses a *spatula* to flip a pancake for her babies. You hold a *shoelace* between your *lips*, trying to tie it with your tongue. You imagine a *sail* boat bobbing in a sea of *milk* and a *pregnant woman* struggling to wrench a *phone charger* from an outlet. Finally, you watch a *cherry* roll across the floor, followed in hot pursuit by your dog, whom you have to tempt away by offering a *biscuit*.

For a list of 20 items or less, you can also double up on your memory words by imagining a block of ice in each image. On item 11, you might picture a lightsaber slicing through an ice cube in your coffee. On item 12, the swan babies could be playing with an ice block while they wait for their pancakes. Repeat this process all the way to number 20, perhaps where Sesame Street's Bert and Ernie (number 10) play hot potato with the block of ice.

Some people love the Number-Shape Method. Others struggle to see how 5 could look like anything but a number. Don't worry if you fall into the second category. There's another method that works just as well for short numbered lists.

Number-Rhyme Method

The *Number-Rhyme Method* is similar to the Number-Shape Method, but associates numbers with rhymes instead of shapes. You might rhyme one with *bun*, two with *shoe*, three with *bee*, four with *floor*, five with *jive*, six with *tricks*, and so on.

Using this method, your first memory word is brought to life with a stale *bun* that you hold over your *travel mug*, hoping the steam will soften it. You use a *spatula* as a makeshift shoe horn to remove your *shoe*. Then, you see a *bee* buzzing around with a *shoelace* tied around its stinger, a wooden *floor* covered in spilled *milk* (yet again), and a dancer rhythmically jerking his thumbs (or *jiving*) with a *phone charger* tied like a bandana around his head. Finally, you watch a magician perform a *trick*, making a *dog biscuit* disappear with her handkerchief.

Can't decide between the Number-Shape or Number-Rhyme Method? Why not combine them for a list of twenty items? You'll benefit from the flexibility of both methods to make your memory words stretch further when you need them to.

Dominic Method

The *Dominic Method*, invented by Dominic O'Brien, is an acronym for Decipherment Of Mnemonically Interpreted Numbers Into Characters. It's similar to the previous two methods, but converts the numbers 00-99 into people and associated actions.

O'Brien (2016) suggests starting off by writing out the numbers and seeing which ones you can already connect with celebrities, historical figures, fictional characters, or people you know personally. For example, you might associate 4 with veteran hockey player Bobby Orr (who wore #4 with the Boston Bruins), 10 with the British Prime Minister (who lives at 10 Downing St), and 27 with any musician who died at that age, like Jimi Hendrix, Kurt Cobain, or Amy Winehouse.

Once you're exhausted your knowledge, return to the numbers that aren't yet associated with a person. Convert these numbers into letters based on this code:

- *O* for 0 (similar shapes)
- *A* for 1 (first letter of the alphabet)
- *B* for 2 (second letter)
- *C* for 3 (third letter)
- *D* for 4 (fourth letter)
- *E* for 5 (fifth letter)
- *S* for 6 (consonant sounds of the number six)
- *G* for 7 (seventh letter)
- *H* for 8 (eighth letter)
- *N* for 9 (consonant sounds of the number nine)

By combining these letters, you substitute two-digit numbers with a series of initials. The next step is to turn these initials into people's names. For example, the number 78 (initials *GH*) might remind you of George Harrison, the guitarist from the Beatles.

The next step is to associate each person with a prop and action. For example, Bobby Orr (4) could fly through the air, similar to his famous 1970 goal. George Harrison (78) could wave from a yellow submarine.

You might want to combine your Dominic code with the Journey Method to make it easier to remember the different points on your journey. This way, you would picture your *mom* (your #1 fan) standing by the coffee *mug* doormat, *Beyoncé* (your association for the letter *B*/number 2) reaching for the *spatula* in the *tree*, and so forth.

You can also use the Dominic Method to memorize a series of numbers, like an important historical date. Simply combine the person from your main code with the prop and action of the number in the corresponding sequence. To remember that the Taj Mahal was completed in 1649, you might picture Molly Ringwald (the lead actress of *Sixteen Candles*) in front of the Taj Mahal stacking poker chips (the action of poker champion Daniel Negreanu, whose initials *DN* make 49).

It may be the most complicated Peg System method to learn, but once you get the hang of it, you can easily apply the Dominic Method to many of your daily memory tasks.

Alphabet Method

The *Alphabet Method* is similar to the previous methods, but lists each item as A to Z instead of 1 to 99. To begin, imagine a concrete object that starts with the sound of each letter, but not necessarily the letter itself. For the letter L, you could use a word like *el*ephant, but not *l*oveseat, for example. If you're struggling to come up with alphabet memory words, try using the first one listed in the dictionary. This way, you can easily look it up if you forget it. Whenever possible, select homophones, like *eye* for I and *jay* for J. Additionally, you can use well-known abbreviations like *WD-40* for W.

Let's say your memory words from A to F are *acorn*, *bee*, *sea*, *dea*con (a Christian priest's second-in-command), *eas*y chair, and *effigy* (a statue or carving of a person). You would imagine your list as an *acorn* bobbing in a *travel mug*, a *bee* flying through the slits of a *spatula*, a *shoelace* tangling with kelp in the *sea*, a *deacon* drinking a carton of *milk* in the middle of mass, a phone charger poking you in the butt when you sit in an *easy chair*, and an *effigy* holding a *dog biscuit* as it burns in a fire.

As an alternative to the sound-based system, you can use *NATO's phonetic alphabet* (O'Brien, 2016). In this case, you would use *alpha*, *bravo*, *Charlie*, etc., as your memory words and incorporate these into your mental images.

The Alphabet Method is slightly less complicated than the Dominic Method, but only allows you to create a list of up to 26 items. However, there is a Peg System method that doesn't require memory words and helps you tackle lists of dozens or even hundreds of items. If you're a fan of BBC's *Sherlock* series, you may already be familiar with it...

Memory Palace Method

The *Memory Palace Method,* also called the "Roman Room Method" or "Mind Palace Method," was popularized in ancient Rome. It involves picturing a room, paying careful attention to the entranceway and the objects and furniture contained within. You then peg your items onto these fixed loci. Boris Nikolai Konrad suggests using a room in your house, but your room can look like whatever you want, as long as it's something you'll remember (TEDx Talks, 2016).

Let's say you're picturing an actual Roman living room. The entranceway might consist of two enormous Corinthian *columns,* with fluted pillars. On your left is an *olive tree,* growing in an urn next to a *table* holding several marble vases. On your right is a *couch* with plump velvet pillows, then a wicker *armchair.* In the centre of the room, there is a *mosaic floor,* dotted with muted red, blue, and green tiles.

Once you've visualized your room, peg any item to any locus you like. You might see a *dog* lying on your *couch* with a *biscuit* in his mouth, a carton of *milk* set among the vases on your *table,* a *shoelace* hanging from the *olive tree,* a *phone charger* draped across the back of the *armchair,* and a *spatula* imprinting more slits into your *columns.* More miraculous yet, the *mosaics* on your *floor* have rearranged to form a *travel mug,* with spirals of steam rising from the top.

Another benefit of the Memory Palace Method is that you can link different rooms together, travelling between them like a true palace. You can also create memories within memories by pegging additional information onto the items you've placed in your room (O'Brien, 2016). It is a method with endless possibilities!

The main downfall of the Memory Palace Method is that it is more difficult to remember numbers than words or images. You could convert your numbers into memory words from the Number-Shape, Number-Rhyme or Dominic Methods. Or, you could turn to the Major System instead, as we'll discuss in the next chapter.

Exercises

Test your mastery of the Link and Peg Systems by memorizing the following:

Forbes' Top 5 Richest Americans (2019): Jeff Bezos, Bill Gates, Warren Buffett, Mark Zuckerbeg, Larry Ellison

The year Karl Benz patented the first modern car: 1886

A bad joke: Did I ever tell you what happened at my Uncle Harvey's funeral? We were at the big church on Main Street with the steep steps. My cousins were the pallbearers. They're all big strong lads, except for Ken. Ken has almost no muscle. But for some reason, someone decided to stick him at the back end of the coffin. So, here they were, carrying Uncle Harvey up these steep steps. They'd almost reached the top when suddenly, Ken let go. The others tried to grab the coffin, but it rolled all the way down the steps of the church. That's not even the worst bit. It soared over the bottom step and flew across the street, with cars blowing their horn and swerving to get out of the way. Miraculously, Uncle Harvey didn't hit anyone. But he did crash through the window of the pharmacy across the street. When he did, the force of the crash opened the lid of the coffin and Uncle Harvey popped out of it. The pharmacist, surprisingly calm, looked up and said, "How can I help you?" And sure as day, Uncle Harvey asked, "Do you have anything to stop this coffin?"

CHAPTER - 05

Mnemonic Systems – Major

The Link and Peg Systems are excellent mnemonic techniques for remembering lists of words. Some of their associated methods, like the Dominic Method, can even help you remember a series of numbers. But what if you aren't familiar with enough celebrities or don't have enough friends and family members to fill the numbers 0 to 99? This is where the *Major System* will come to your rescue.

This system works on a similar principle to the Dominic Method, using a special code to replace the numbers zero to nine with consonant sounds. Buzan (2006) provides the following code (p. 76):

- 0 becomes *s* or *z* (like the first sound in zero)
- 1 becomes *d*, *t*, or *th* (all letters with one downstroke)
- 2 becomes *n* (two downstrokes)
- 3 becomes *m* (three downstrokes)
- 4 becomes *r* (the last letter in the word four)
- 5 becomes *l* – (Roman numeral 50)
- 6 becomes *j* or *sh* (the cursive j is almost a mirror image of the number 6)
- 7 becomes *k*, *ch*, *g*, *ng* (like ki*ng* or *g*nocchi), or *qu* (capital Ks look like interlocking number 7s)
- 8 becomes *f* or *v* (the cursive f has two loops, like the number 8)
- 9 becomes *b* or *p* (mirror images of the number 9)

By substituting numbers for letters, you can use free vowels to combine them into a memory word. For example, you could associate the 29 with *n* and *p* and add the letter A to create *nap*. To remember the number 29, simply picture someone or something taking a nice long *nap*.

The Major System also works well for memorizing important dates, like birthdays and anniversaries. Let's say your partner's birthday is September 29th. Using your *nap* memory word, you would also substitute September (the ninth month) with the number 9 and get the word *bay*. Picture your partner taking a *nap* by a *bay* window or along the shores of a peaceful *bay* and you'll never forget to buy them a card on their special day.

You can easily use the Major System to create a list up to the number 1000 (*these zoos*). If you're feeling ambitious, you can even create four- or five-consonant words, like *telephone* for 1582 and *flamenco* for 85327. Or, you could expand your three-digit repertoire by using the *Multiplier Method*, as we'll discuss in the next section.

Multiplier Method

This offshoot of the Major System helps you memorize up to 1000 additional digits by adding extra details to your memory images. These consist of your original memory word...

- Along with a block of ice for the numbers 1000-1999
- Covered in thick oil for 2000-2999
- Engulfed in flames for 3000-3999
- As a brilliant shade of purple for 4000-4999
- As a velvet imprint fOr 5000-5999
- As a transparent figure for 6000-6999
- Imbibed with your favorite scent for 7000-7999
- Along a busy road for 8000-8999
- On top of a fluffy cloud floating in a beautiful sunny sky for 9000-10000

The beauty of the Multiplier Method is that by adding these details, you can expand your list of memory words without adding extra consonants. For example, if you wanted to stick to three-consonant memory words, instead of the telephone example from the last section, you could remember the number 1582 as a group of hippies having a *love-in* (memory word for 582) in a *block of ice* (the multiplier for the digit 1).

You could also take your five-consonant memory words and expand them into six-digit territory with this same system. Let's say the number you want to memorize is 985327. You can accomplish this by picturing a *flamenco* dancer (memory word for 85327) performing a Sevillana step on top of a fluffy *cloud* floating in a beautiful *sunny sky* (the multiplier for the digit 9).

Additionally, you could apply the Multiplier Method to other mnemonic methods. As mentioned in Chapter 4, the *block of ice* multiplier detail can be added to the Number-Shape and the Number-Rhyme Methods to expand your memory words for the numbers 11-20.

You can also incorporate the other multiplier details to expand your list right up to the number 100. For example, for the number 34, you could picture either a *sailboat* (your number-shape for the number 4) or a linoleum *floor* (your number-rhyme for the number 4) engulfed in *flames* (your multiplier for 3).

With so many possibilities, it's no wonder that the Multiplier Method is a favorite addition to many other mnemonic systems.

Long Number Method

The Multiplier Method may work well for four-, five-, and even six-digit numbers. But what if you want to remember a number with seven or more digits? The good news is you can still use the basic principles of the Major System by breaking your number into chunks of two or three digits.

Let's say you want to memorize the first eight decimal values of pi: 14159265. Break it into chunks and you get the numbers 14, 15, 92, and 65.

For each of these numbers, your Major System code might give you the following memory words: *dear, doll, pan,* and *shell.* Imagine a *dear* porcelain *doll,* with curly hair and a floral petticoat, in a toy kitchen. She takes a *pan* and fills it with a pastry *shell* to bake a pie for dessert. By picturing this image, you'll not only remember the numbers themselves. You'll also connect them to their proper mathematical concept, thanks to the homophone *pi* (the value)/*pie* (the food).

If you're having trouble visualizing all of these memory words, you can always combine the Long Number Method with a Peg System method. For example, if you can't remember the word *shell* for the number 65, imagine the *dear doll* taking the pie out of the *pan,* placing a *cherry* (the number-shape for 6) on top and serving it to a *jive* dancer (the number-rhyme for 5). You could also peg these items in your Memory Palace by setting the *doll* on the *armchair,* a *pan* beneath the *olive tree,* and a *deer* (slight homophone change) on the *couch,* while imagining *shell* shapes decorating your *mosaic floor.*

It takes a lot of dedication to master the Long Number Method. Yet, the payoff is well worth it. Not only will it improve your memory: it will also boost your IQ. According to Buzan (2006), the average person can only remember a number with 6-7 digits. Yet, if you can remember 9 or more on an IQ test, that will put you in the 150+ range!

Even if you don't subscribe to the IQ test as a true measure of intelligence, the Long Number Method can still help you sharpen your verbal, spatial, and logical-numerical smarts to improve your long-term memory.

Major/Acrostic Method

Buzan (2006) describes two different methods for remembering telephone numbers and important historical dates. Yet, they all work on the same principle, by combining the principles of the Major System code with the simple mnemonic effectiveness of acrostics.

You could always use the Long Number Method for telephone numbers and basic Major System for dates. Still, it isn't always easy to find a single memory word or set of three to four memory words to successfully substitute for these numbers. The benefit of the Major/Acrostic hybrid method is that it gives you the freedom to create memorable sentences, whose topics are often associated with the meaning of the numbers themselves.

Let's say you want to remember the number of your company's New York office. The number is: 212-493-4781.

Using your Major System code, you would get letters that look something like this: N D N- R B M - R CH F T. Because this is a work number, you'll want to come up with an acrostic that is somehow work-related, such as "No, I Don't Need Reminding of my Boss's Many Reasons for CHanging Filing Tabs." You can even incorporate the names of coworkers, projects, and other work jargon to help jog your memory.

You can also use the Major/Acrostic Method to remember important historical dates. For example, the Spanish conquistador Francisco Pizarro defeated the Inca Empire in 1533. Using your Major System code, you end up with the letters D L M M. The acrostic Don't Let Mummies be Murdered not only reminds you of this important date, it also reminds you that Pizarro's men cruelly destroyed the sacred mummies of past rulers in order to dominate the Inca people.

Once you've mastered the Major System code, you'll notice how easy it is to combine it with other mnemonics to help you remember important numbers. Yet, it isn't just numbers that the Major System can help you remember. It works just as well as the Journey Method for memorizing cards.

Card Memory Method

The Card Memory Method is popular with magicians, gamblers, memory champs, and anyone else who wishes to memorize a pack of playing cards in the order that they're called out (Figure 9). It works on the same principle as the Major System, but with a twist.

Figure 9: The Card Memory Method is a hit at parties. Not so much at casinos (Wong, 2017).

You begin by taking the first letter of the name of the card's suit, such as *c* for clubs or *d* for diamonds. For cards 2 through 9, substitute the number of the card with the consonant from the Major System code and create a memory word for each combination. For example, your memory word for the 3 of diamonds might be *dam*, because it combines the *d* of diamond with the *m* code for the number 3.

For aces, 10s, and the face cards, you'll first have to substitute them with (other) numbers before you convert them to the Major code. Aces become 1s, 1os becomes 0s, jacks become 11s, and queens become 12s. Kings are the easiest to remember, because you only have to take the name of their suit. For instance, your memory word for the king of hearts is simply "heart."

The Card Memory Method may sound complicated. Yet, once you've successfully established your memory words, you'll find that it's quite easy to combine them with your existing Major System code.

Let's say the first card to be called is the 7 of spades. Your Card Method memory word for spades + 7 might be *sack*, while your Major System code word for the number 1 might be *tea*. In this case, imagine Santa Claus opening up his toy *sack*, only to have a deluge of *tea* come spilling out. Similarly, if the second card is the queen of clubs and your number 2 code word is *no*, you might imagine a *cotton* ball with a red X through it.

By repeating this process for all 52 cards and developing strong mental images for each one, you'll surprise yourself by how easily you can recall them once someone asks you to repeat the sequence.

Even if you're not interested in memorizing cards, there are plenty of other mnemonic techniques that can help you overcome memory challenges in various, everyday situations. We'll discuss these task-specific techniques in greater detail in the next chapter.

Exercises

Test your knowledge of the Major System by memorizing the following:

The number of bones in the human body: 206

Isaac Newton's birthday: January 4th

The "phoenix number" (whose first six multiples are anagrams): 142, 857

Your florist's phone number: 894-9932

The year of Brown vs. Board of Education: 1954

A card sequence: three of diamonds, ace of clubs, king of hearts, seven of diamonds, ten of spades

CHAPTER - 06

Task-Specific Mnemonic Techniques

The different systems and methods described in Chapters 4 and 5 may be effective for certain tasks, like memorizing a grocery list or recalling historical dates. But what if you need to remember a binary computer code, where you can't easily substitute the same number-shapes over and over again? Or what if you need to rehearse for a big presentation that has too many detours for the Journey Method to handle? Maybe you'd like to learn how to figure out the day of the week for all the dates from the year 1800? Or at least you'd like to remember where you left your keys and wallet?

The good news is there are easy-to-learn mnemonic techniques that can help you adopt fast, efficient, and successful ways of completing these tasks outlined above. We'll also learn some other task-specific mnemonics, from remembering names and faces to successfully translating Spanish words.

Calculating Days of the Week

O'Brien (2016) provides a rather complicated technique for calculating days of the week. It takes some getting used to, but once you've mastered it, you'll be able to link it to any date from from the year 1800 to 2099!

This technique is a hybrid method. It combines elements of the Dominic Method, Memory Palace Method, and Number-Shape Method, along with your own individual powers of association. It helps to write everything down at the beginning until your brain gets used to cracking the code and making these associations automatically.

On a basic level, the formula is Year Code + Month Code + Date Number = Day Code. These Day Codes all correspond to a day of the week, from Sunday to Saturday.

Let's say that you'd like to know what day of the week November 6th 1978 fell on.

You would begin by taking six rooms from your Memory Palace, plus a yard or garden to serve as the number 0. Let's say your six rooms, in order from 1 to 6, are your *living room*, *dining room*, *kitchen*, *bathroom*, *bedroom*, and *study*. You can also use the Number-Shape Method to help you associate each room with its proper number. For example, you might picture a *lightsaber* suspended on the wall of your *living room*, a *swan* centrepiece on your *dining room* table, and so on.

Next, you'll need to write the years 1900 to 1999 in seven columns, each labelled with your corresponding room (or yard). Beginning in the yard column, write the year 1900. In your living room column, write the year 1901. In your dining room write the year

1902, and so on, returning to the yard for the year 1907. Repeat this distribution of years across your rooms until you reach the year 1999.

Then, take the final two digits of each year and connect them to your memorable person, prop, and action from your Dominic code. Don't forget to imagine this person in the corresponding room of your Memory Palace! For the year 1978, you might picture George Harrison in his yellow submarine floating in your study. This will link the year 1978 to the number 6 (associated with your study). Therefore, 6 is your Year Code.

Before we move on to the Month Code, it's worth discussing some extra factors to keep in mind while calculating your Year Code. If your year is a leap year, you'll need to subtract 1 from your Year Code if your date falls between January 1st and February 29th. One easy way to remember this is that a leap year occurs every four years. If you divide the last two digits of your year by four and end up with a non-decimal number, then you'll know it's a leap year. For example, $78 \div 4 = 19.5$. Therefore, 1978 was not a leap year. However, 1980 was a leap year, because $80 \div 4 = 20$. The only exception to this rule is for the first year of the century. A leap year only occurs in this instance if the first two digits are a multiple of four. Therefore, the years 1800 and 1900 did not contain a leap year, but the year 2000 did.

Finally, to calculate years from the year 1800 to 1899 or 2000 to 2099, you'll need to add a Century Code. Simply calculate your Year Code as you would for a 20th-century date, but add 2 for the 19th-century dates and 6 for the 21st-century dates.

Let's go back to 1978, where we've learned that the Year Code is 6. The next step is to figure out your Month Code. It might be easier for you to memorize the numbers associated with each month instead of coming up with another mnemonic. Yet, if you find it difficult, you can adopt memory words, simple rhymes, puns, or any other techniques to help you memorize them. Here are the Month Codes:

- January is 1 (think of the *first month*)
- February is 4 (same first letter as the number *four*)
- March is 4 (think of *march*ing *forward*)
- April is 0 (think of *raindrops* from *April* showers)
- May is 2 (think of *two* possibilities: you *may* or *may* not)
- June is 5 (think of a *pregnant lady*, your *5* number-shape, and name her *June*)
- July is 0 (*Jul* rhymes with *null*, another word for *zero*)
- August is 3 (think of *a gust* of wind, knocking over *three* beach umbrellas)

> September is 6 (think of a *cherry*, the 6 number-shape, carrying a backpack with back-to-school supplies)

> October is 1 (picture a trick-or-treater in a Jedi costume carrying a *lightsaber*)

> November is 4 (picture a *war veteran*, associated with November 11th, on a *sailboat*, your 4 number-shape)

> December is 6 (think of *six geese a-laying*, from the *12 Days of Christmas*)

Since our date is in November, we'll add the Month Code 4 to our Year Code 6, getting 6 + 4 = 10. Add this to the number 6 (our date of the month) and we get 6 + 4 + 6 = 16.

Finally, you'll need to memorize the Day Codes. These are much easier to remember, because they are ordered 0-6, with Saturday represented as Code 0 and Friday represented as Code 6. To figure out this Day Code, simply subtract as many 7s as you can without going into the negatives.

For our November 6th 1978 total, which is 16, we would subtract 16-7 = 9. We would subtract 9 minus 7 again to get 2, which is the Day Code for Monday. Therefore, November 6th 1978 fell on a Monday.

Of course, this technique is a lot more complicated than Googling the calendar dates for the year 1978. But mastering it will exercise your brain, improve your memory, and enhance your logical-mathematical, verbal, and spatial skills. You'll also have a new skill to impress your friends at your next get-together.

Remembering Binary Numbers

It may not be quite as impressive as your day-of-the-week calculations, but another potential party trick is to show off how well you can remember a sequence of binary numbers. Even if your guests don't appreciate the subtle art of memorization, this technique can still be useful for remembering computer code.

To begin, O'Brien (2016) suggests breaking down your sequence into three-digit numbers. Each of these combinations can be substituted with the single-digital numbers 0-7. Again, you can use your own mnemonic techniques to remember this code:

> 000 becomes 0. Think *zero* number ones

> 001 becomes 1. Think *one* number 1 (Roman numeral I)

> 011 becomes 2. Think *two* number 1s (Roman numeral II)

- 111 becomes 3. Think *three* number 1s (Romans numeral III)
- 110 becomes 4. Picture *two* babies (1 and 1) hatched from a fertilized egg (0), which was created by *two* parents
- 100 becomes 5. Picture using opera glasses (the 1 is the stick, the 0s are the lenses) to look at a *jive* dancer (number-rhyme for 5)
- 010 becomes 6. Picture a wide-eyed person (the 0s are eyes, the 1 is a nose) watching magic *tricks* (number-rhyme for 6)
- 101 becomes 7. Picture a dinner plate (the 0) set with a fork and knife (the two 1s), a true food lover's heaven (number-rhyme for 7)

You can then combine two three-digit groups and their associated 1-7 numbers into your Dominic code. For example, the number 001101 can be split into 001 and 101, which become 1 and 7, which become 17. You might think of the rock star Stevie Nicks, who sang the song "Edge of *Seventeen.*" If the following six-digit number was 111010, you would get the number 36, which might be your code for *CS* (36) Lewis, the author of the Chronicles of Narnia series. Picture Stevie Nicks riding Aslan the lion, and you've just associated the sequence 001101111010 with a single, memorable image.

Like the Days of the Week calculation, this mnemonic technique requires dedicated practice, along with comfortable knowledge of basic mnemonics, along with the Dominic Method. The Dominic Method, along with the other Peg System methods, may still seem a bit confusing.

Yet, if you've mastered the basic Link System and Journey Method, you're in luck. Both of these techniques can be successfully applied to learning foreign language words, as we'll discover in the next section.

LinkWord Technique/Town Language Mnemonic

To memorize words from other languages, mnemonic experts provide two closely related techniques: the *LinkWord Technique* and the *Town Language Mnemonic*.

The LinkWord Technique is similar to the basic Link System, but incorporates verbal word associations to cement your translations in place (Memory Techniques – Learning Foreign Languages, n.d.). All you have to do is associate a word from your language with the foreign word you want to learn, then create a strong mental image to remember it. For example, the Spanish word for bread is *pan*. To remember this translation, imagine taking freshly baked *bread* out of the oven and setting the *pan* on the stove. You can also substitute words with no English homophone for the nearest English equivalent. For the Spanish word *zapatos*, which means *shoes*, imagine that you're playing cops and robbers with a young boy. He sneaks up behind you, points the gun at your *shoes* and *zaps at* your *toes*. The LinkWord Technique may seem a bit juvenile, since it relies on so many puns. Yet, it's actually a respected mnemonic technique that linguists recommend to help you learn new languages.

The Town Language Mnemonic combines elements of the LinkWord Technique with the Journey Method to create an organized dictionary for all your language translations (O'Brien, 2016). It's based on the fact that common vocabulary in any language is related to everyday people, objects, places, and events. To start, choose a town or city that you're familiar with and start associating loci with foreign words. Imagine nouns around town, like *libro* (book) as a dusty red tome on a shelf at the library and *pájaro* (bird) as a fat pigeon on the head of the statue in the town square. In a gendered language like Spanish, you can also divide your city into gendered zones, like masculine nouns west of the river and feminine nouns east of the river. Or, you could imagine two separate towns, placing masculine nouns in one and feminine nouns in the other.

Once you've placed your nouns around your city or cities, it's time to add the adjectives and verbs. Associate adjectives with parks, where your senses come alive as you see flower beds that are *bonita* (pretty), hear ultimate frisbee players that are *rudioso* (noisy), and smell lilac trees that are *calmante* (soothing). Finally, imagine verbs in a gym or outdoor field, where you can *caminar* (walk), *correr* (run), and *jugar beisbol* (play baseball).

Once you've mastered the basic vocabulary, you can 'move' to a different town or city to learn another language. Or, if the languages are different enough from each other, you may be able to successfully layer multiple language words onto the same journey. For example, it might be too difficult to add Italian adjectives like *bella* (pretty), *rumoroso* (noisy), and *calmante* (soothing) to your Spanish town, because they are both Romance languages and share many similar words. This problem becomes less pronounced in a Celtic language like Irish, where you can easily distinguish words like álainn (pretty), *callánach* (noisy), and *suaimhneasach* (soothing).

Like the previous techniques from this chapter, the LinkWord technique and Town Language Mnemonic both require some knowledge of the concepts we discussed in Chapter 4. Yet, not all task-specific mnemonics require a working knowledge of a complex mnemonic system. For the remainder of this chapter, we'll be focusing on simple mnemonic techniques that are built on the basic visual and verbal concepts we learned in Chapter 3.

Social Etiquette Method

Remembering names and faces can be a daunting challenge, especially when you meet a room full of new people at the same time. Yet, as Buzan (2006) argues, his Social Etiquette Method can help demystify names and faces, allowing you to interact with them with greater ease (Figure 10).

The first step of the Social Etiquette Method is to relax and take an interest in the person you're meeting. It will be much more difficult to remember them if your mind is too busy stressing over the situation or wandering to other places.

The next step is to look the person directly in the eye and take note of their facial features. What shape is their head? What does their nose look like? What color are their eyes and how close are they together? Do they have a double chin? Do they have a distinct hairstyle? Do they have facial hair? Taking note of these distinct traits will help you recognize them whenever you meet again.

When they introduce themselves, listen closely to the sound of the person's name. Even if you have heard it, ask them to repeat it and repeat it yourself out loud, making sure you've pronounced it correctly. Ask them to spell it if you're still not sure. Harrison & Hobbs (2010) also suggest looking for associations that you can make with their name. For example, if you're a classic rock fan and you meet someone named Angie, you can associate her with the Rolling Stones song. Similarly, O'Brien (2016) suggests associating this person with a place where you might run into them. For example, if Angie works in a library, you might make this connection by imagining Mick Jagger serenading her in front of a shelf of encyclopedias.

Figure 10: The Social Etiquette Method makes it much easier to remember names and faces (Cytonn Photography, 2018).

As you continue your conversation with this person, use their name as often as you can. Saying things like "Tell me, Ugo, what is it like to work in publishing?" or "Gurinder, I'd like you to meet my sister..." will reinforce their name in your memory as you repeat it over and over. It also helps to repeat the person's name in your head whenever there's a pause in conversation or after your conversation ends and you see them from another corner of the room.

It may be tempting to learn as many names as you can and as quickly possible. Yet, by taking your time with each person, you'll be much more likely to commit them to memory. It takes some practice, but you'll soon find yourself mastering the names of a whole group of people in one setting.

Mind Mapping

Now that you've mastered the art of learning names and faces, you'll be able to confidently greet everyone by name at your next big pitch or keynote speech. Yet, what about the pitch or speech itself? How will you remember all of your main points and supporting information to share in front of Angie, Ugo, and Gurinder?

Have no fear! *Mind maps* are here.

This mnemonic technique, invented by Tony Buzan, combines words and images to visualize information, with clear connections between ideas (Buzan & Harrison, 2010). To start, draw your key word or image in the centre of your paper, then add a series of colorful branch-like lines to connect other words or images as points and subpoints. Don't overthink this step. Simply just jot down the first word or image that comes to mind and see where it leads you. It's also important to limit your key words and images to one per line to maximize the potential associations you can make.

For example, if you were pitching an idea for a new video-sharing app, you might start with the name of the app or simply "Video-Sharing App" if you haven't yet decided on the name. You can then add branches connecting to the app's features, UI (user interface), compatible devices, and so on.

You can also keep your Mind Map organized by underlining the most important words, color coding themes, adding arrows, and numbering branches in order of greatest importance. For an unnamed app, you might want to add a branch for your name category, then list potential choices in order of preference.

After creating your mind map and looking it over a few times, you'll find that it's much easier to remember all of your talking points for your presentation.

The beauty of mind mapping is that it's highly flexible. You can use it to take lecture notes, plan essays, manage team projects, and decide on everyday courses of action by analyzing the pros and cons, and causes and effects of each option. It's a mnemonic technique that not only jogs your memory, but also keeps you organized.

Yet, even the most organized people forget things at times, like where they left their work boots or whether or not they changed their cat's litter. Unfortunately, mind mapping, like the other mnemonics discussed so far, probably won't be of much use in these situations. Still, there is one more technique that might just solve the mystery.

Reliving the Immediate Relevant Past

According to Buzan (2006), the Reliving the Immediate Relevant Past technique helps you remember the things you have forgotten by focusing on associated objects and experiences that you can remember. It aims to create a loose, unstructured *stream of consciousness*, allowing your thoughts to flow freely at rapid speed until they stumble upon the forgotten memory.

Let's say that you've lost your keys. You know that they're somewhere in your house, because you used them to return from your trip to the post office a couple of hours ago. Instead of panicking and focusing on the lost keys themselves, keep a cool head and start thinking of features, objects, and actions associated with your keys. Visualize what your keys look like, where you usually put your keys, what you see when you first walk in the door, what jacket or bag you brought outside with you, and what shoes you wore when you left. Picture every room you've been in over the last couple hours, including what you did in each one. It might help to retrace your steps at this point, performing your most recent actions in chronological order.

When you focus on these associations and let your mind flow freely, it will be much easier to remember where you left your keys or any other object you may have forgotten. It may take a while. It may even come to you in the middle of the night when your mind is at its least inhibited. Yet, training yourself to repeat these steps whenever you lose something will eventually make the process go much faster.

You can also use the Reliving the Immediate Relevant Past technique for lost thoughts, like when you forget what you were about to say to a friend. After letting them know, ask them to help you recreate what you had just talked about, trying to remember everything verbatim. Let your mind flow freely as you hear each word, creating as many associations as you can. Once again, with the right amount of practice, you'll soon find yourself re-remembering these thoughts mere seconds after they slip away from you.

This concludes our discussion of mnemonic techniques. In the next chapter, we'll focus on more indirect tips, tricks, and activities to help you improve your memory.

Exercises

Test your new task-specific skills by completing the following:

Calculate the day of the week of America's bicentennial: July 4th, 1976

Memorize this binary code: 000101111011

Learn these Japanese words (spelled phonetically): *arigato* (thank you), *sakana* (fish), *kazoku* (family), *kakkoi* (cool), *yabai* (terrible)

Remember the following people: Miguel (tall, lawyer, plays drums), Shannon (curly red hair, podcaster, vegan), Yasmin (wrist tattoo, preschool teacher, loves gardening), Sanjay (baseball cap, architect, volunteer firefighter)

Create a mind map for a presentation on your favorite movie

Figure out where you left your phone, wallet, keys, and favorite shoes

CHAPTER - 07

Memory-Boosting Tips, Tricks, and Hobbies

While you're hard at work learning the mnemonic devices, systems, and methods from the last few chapters, why not adopt some new ways to improve your memory indirectly? They take much less conscious effort than creating an acronym or developing your Dominic Code, but they still hold many benefits for boosting your memory.

In the first half of this chapter, we'll discuss some general tips for reading, writing, studying, and reviewing in order to maximize your memory potential. In the second half, we'll learn about some fun activities that can boost your memory, like abstract painting, solving Sudokus, and even playing video games.

Memory-Friendly Tips and Tricks

Maybe you're learning how to boost your memory to help you in school or at work. Or maybe you're just learning for fun at home. Either way, there are several ways you can expand your memory simply by changing the way you read texts, take notes, learn new words, and review what you've recently learned.

Reading Texts

Many of us were taught that to maximize our memory for what texts we've read, we should read as slowly as we can, taking time to analyze each word. Yet, many memory experts argue that slow reading is more time-consuming and less effective overall than speed reading.

Speed reading helps you improve your concentration by focusing your brain on a singular, fast-paced task (Buzan & Harrison, 2010). You may not read each individual word, but you can better retain the information as a whole by focusing on the most important points and committing them to memory.

Although the average person only reads 200-240 words per minute, it is possible to increase your rate to over 500 words per minute. All you need are the right methods and the dedication to keep on improving.

When you start speed reading, it's important to use your finger or some sort of pointer, like a pen or stylus, as a guide. This is because it's much easier for your eyes to follow a moving object than stare at an unmoving page. Start with a *double-line sweep*, using your pointer to sweep across two lines from left to right, move back to the left for the following two lines, and so on. Once you have mastered this, try the *variable sweep*, which takes in a greater number of lines per sweep, and the *reverse sweep*, which moves from right to left. This last one is especially effective for remembering individual words, because it works against our natural order for reading text in the English world. After attempting all three sweeps, you can choose the one that works best for you.

Using your peripheral vision will help you visualize a greater amount of words at a single time rather than zeroing in on a small concentration of words. This also reduces eye strain, enabling you to read for longer periods. To increase your field of vision, try holding your reading material at least 20 inches from your eyes and adjusting your font and window size so that the lines cover your entire laptop or tablet screen.

When you're speed reading, it's tempting to backtrack and re-read words, but try to keep going as quickly as you can. Once you adjust to a faster speed of reading, you'll be able to confidently find your rhythm without ever needing to return to previous paragraphs.

For some people, vocalizing words as you read them can slow you down. Yet, especially for dyslexics and non-native English speakers, it can actually help you concentrate on the text and reinforce what you're reading. Additionally, fMRI scans show that reading out loud engages memory areas in both hemispheres of the brain (Harrison & Hobbs, 2010). Therefore, by combining your vocalizations with your speed reading, you can rest assured that your hard work will pay off when you remember exactly what you've read.

Writing Notes

As we've discussed in previous chapters, writing down acronyms, acrostics, mnemonic codes, and mind maps can be a great way to trigger your visual memory. Yet, the benefits of handwriting don't end there.

Even when you're writing a regular list or a series of lecture notes without any mnemonic techniques, studies show that writing by hand will help you remember information better than typing on a computer (Smoker et al., 2009). This is because handwriting is a complex motor skill that engages your muscle memory as well as your verbal memory. Writing by hand also encourages you to be more conscious of your spelling and grammar, since you're not relying on a spellcheck feature to detect mistakes automatically. This, in turn, will boost your memory for language conventions.

It's also important to write notes in your own words instead of copying them verbatim from another source. When you draw on the vocabulary you know well, it becomes much easier to memorize and understand new concepts.

One exception to this is when you're trying to expand your vocabulary with new words. As we will learn in the following section, it helps to use these unfamiliar words as often as you can in order to commit them to long-term memory.

Learning Words

Though most languages are made up of over 3 million words, the average person only speaks about 1000 words in their everyday vocabulary (Buzan, 2006; Harrison & Hobbs, 2010). We often write more words than these and understand the meanings of even more words. Yet when we make a conscious effort to expand our vocabulary, we are able to speak more articulately, think more critically, and understand more complex ideas. This not only boosts our overall intelligence, it also enables us to remember things much easier.

There are two main methods you can use to expand your vocabulary. The first method is introducing at least one new word into your vocabulary each day. Use your word as often as possible throughout your day and across the week in order to transfer it to your long-term memory. Many online dictionaries, apps, and 365-day calendars offer a "Word of the Day" feature. Alternately, you can open a print dictionary, flip to a random page, and choose the first unknown word that you see.

The second is reading the dictionary to learn important prefixes and suffixes, along with Latin, Greek, and Germanic word roots that form the majority of words in modern English. Learning these will help you decipher the meaning of new words, even if you've never heard them before. For example, you may not know what the word *antediluvian* means at first glance. Yet, if you know that the prefix *ante–* means 'before,' the suffix *-ian* means 'from' or "characteristic of," and the Latin root *diluvium* means 'deluge,' you can correctly guess that the word is an adjective that describes something "before the deluge." In this case, it is a figurative term for something quite ancient, pre-dating the Biblical flood described in the Book of Genesis.

Learning these building blocks of the English language is also useful when learning other Indo-European languages, especially from the Romance and Germanic families. For example, knowing the meaning of the Latin root word *diluvium* helps you understand the meaning of *diluvio* in Spanish and Italian ('flood'). Similarly, knowing the meaning of the Old English root word *flōwan* ("to flow") will help you remember the meaning of the German *Flut* ('flood') and the Swedish *flod* ('river'). It may not always be an exact translation from English, but it can at least point you in the right direction.

Now that you've learned some new words, the key is to find ways to commit them to your long-term memory. The more you practice them, the more likely you'll remember them. This is all true of studying techniques, as we'll learn in the next section.

Reviewing Concepts

Just as pianists must play a song over and over to commit it to muscle memory, so you must regularly review new material to commit it to your long-term memory. By reviewing new words, concepts, and ideas, you create new synaptic connections in your brain that strengthen your memory and increase your likelihood of recall.

The key to successful reviewing is knowing how often to look over new information and how to organize your notes. Without regular reviewing, most people can only remember 20% of the information they have learned in a 24-hour period (Buzan & Harrison, 2010; Harrison & Hobbs, 2010). Therefore, experts recommend that students should maximize their retention by reviewing lecture materials once after class, once later that day, then on a regular basis, whenever they find themselves forgetting what they have learned. This may range from a weekly to monthly to tri-monthly basis. Every memory is different, so you may have to do some experimenting until you find the method that works best for you. One you figure out your formula, you can apply this to all of your learning, whether in the classroom, at the office, at home, or around town.

The next step is to use techniques that ease the retrieval stage of memory. Our brains are always searching for patterns that make new information easier to remember. Mnemonic techniques exploit this hardwired function to create associations between new information and known words, images, and concepts. Yet, even something as simple as creating an ordered list can increase your likelihood of remembering the information. For instance, a scattered list of numbers like 8 5 2 4 9 might be difficult to remember compared to an ascending order like 2 4 5 8 9. It is also easier to remember words in alphabetical order, dates in chronological order, and so on.

Mind maps lend themselves well to this type of ordered, patterned reviewing. Yet, instead of always reviewing the same mind map, try creating a brand new map during each study session. This will test how well you remember ideas from your original map. You may even come up with new information along the way.

Now that we've covered some memory-friendly tips for reading, writing, and studying, let's take a look at some everyday activities and hobbies that can also boost your memory.

Memory-Friendly Hobbies

Aside from dedicated brain training techniques, you can improve your memory by exercising your creative thinking, concentration powers, and critical skills with everyday activities. These include dream journaling, drawing and painting, meditating, solving puzzles, charting your own maps, and playing video games. You'll be so busy enjoying yourself, you probably won't even notice how hard your brain is working or how fast your memory is improving!

Unless noted otherwise, the information in this section has been adopted from Harrison & Hobbs (2010).

Dream Journals

Whether they come in the middle of the night while you're fast asleep or the middle of the day while you're zoning out at work, dreams are a memorable source of weird, wacky, and wonderful ideas. Many of the best creative minds were inspired by their dreams, like Edgar Allan Poe for his nightmarish short stories and Salvador Dali for his absurd, surrealist paintings.

Studies show that when we remember our dreams, we become calmer, more motivated, and less forgetful of other things. So, many people turn to dream journaling as a way to gather their creative energies and improve their memories in the process.

However, it can be difficult to add lavish descriptions and free-hand sketches to a journal when you're in the habit of forgetting dreams. That's why Buzan (2006) suggests repeating a mantra to yourself as you begin to fall asleep: "I will remember my dream, I will remember my dream, I will remember my dream" (p. 172). It may take a few weeks, but eventually, your brain will start to give in.

As soon as you wake up, try using the Journey Method or any other mnemonic method to associate two or three key images from your dream. For example, you might use the Alphabet Method to remember a dream where you saw a wizard in long, flowing robes and a pointed hat riding a sheep across a meadow filled with seedy dandelions. In this case, you would imagine the wizard balancing an *acorn* atop his hat, the sheep darting playfully after a *bee*, and the dandelions forming an endless *sea*.

Once you get into the hang of remembering your dreams, you'll be surprised by just how easily forgotten things come to mind.

Drawing and Painting

What do American actress Rita Hayworth, Dutch artist Willem de Kooning, and sawmill worker Lester Potts have in common? They all turned to painting as a way to cope with dementia (Chancellor, et al. 2014).

Art therapy, which uses painting and drawing to promote well-being, was first invented to help people suffering from cancer and post-traumatic stress disorders. More recently, it's been used to treat patients in early or middle stages of dementia. Although the art they create tends to be abstract with fewer and muted colors, it helps many patients feel calm and in control of their emotions. Additionally, it's a powerful memory boost, with up to 78% of art therapy patients able to draw or paint from memory at least some of the time.

Even for people without dementia, creating art can help you become more engaged and in touch with your emotions. This is why neurologists often ask people to copy abstract art to test their memory and attention span.

You don't need to be able to sketch like Picasso or paint like Salvador Dali to start creating art. Simply pick up your canvas or sketchpad and begin. Whether it's a detailed landscape of your favorite camping spot, a crudely drawn portrait of your pet, or a violent array of paint splatters, let yourself go and let your hand do the thinking. When you regularly unleash your creativity without limits, you'll be surprised by how much more agile your thinking becomes.

Meditation

Although it's been a vital practice in Eastern religions for millennia, the western world is only just waking up to the power of meditation. It is an exercise that aims to calm the mind and reach a state of 'nonthinking' by focusing on a mantra, sound, or pattern of breathing. Buddhists see meditation as a rigorous form of mental training that frees your mind from hatred, jealousy, and other vices, and opens your heart to compassion. Others see it as a non-religious, mindful activity that can reduce negative thoughts, lower stress, and help you feel relaxed.

Recent cognitive studies show that when you meditate regularly, your prefrontal cortex thickens. This increases your attention and improves your sensory processing. Over time, it can completely rewire the neurons in your brain, reducing the release of stress hormones and even relieving the effects of depression.

To start, find a quiet space where you can sit down with your back straight, unsupported by a wall or cushion. Close your eyes or focus them on a fixed object, like a candle flame or a mandala design. As you do this, breath deeply. Pay attention to the rhythm of your breaths, allowing each inhale to fill your chest and each exhale to fill your mouth. If you want, you can repeat a chant like 'om' or "don't worry" either out loud or in your head. Aim to keep breathing and repeating your mantra for at least five minutes.

Once you become a regular meditator, you may wish to extend your meditations for as long as an hour. But for now, try it in bite-sized increments, seeing for how long you can maintain your focus.

If you have trouble keeping your hands still, you can put them to good use during your meditation practices by tapping or massaging them into your K-27 points. These are the shallow, finger-sized indentations in your chest slightly down and inward from your collarbone. Concentrating on these points while breathing has been shown to clear your mind and increase your energy post-meditation.

Puzzles

Puzzles are a fun way to improve your problem solving skills, while having fun in the process. Jigsaw puzzles have been shown to benefit your spatial memory (Figure 11). Plus, they help clear your mind of daily stresses as you focus on assembling a picture in front of you, piece by piece. Best of all, once you're finished, you'll have a lovely work of art to show for your labors.

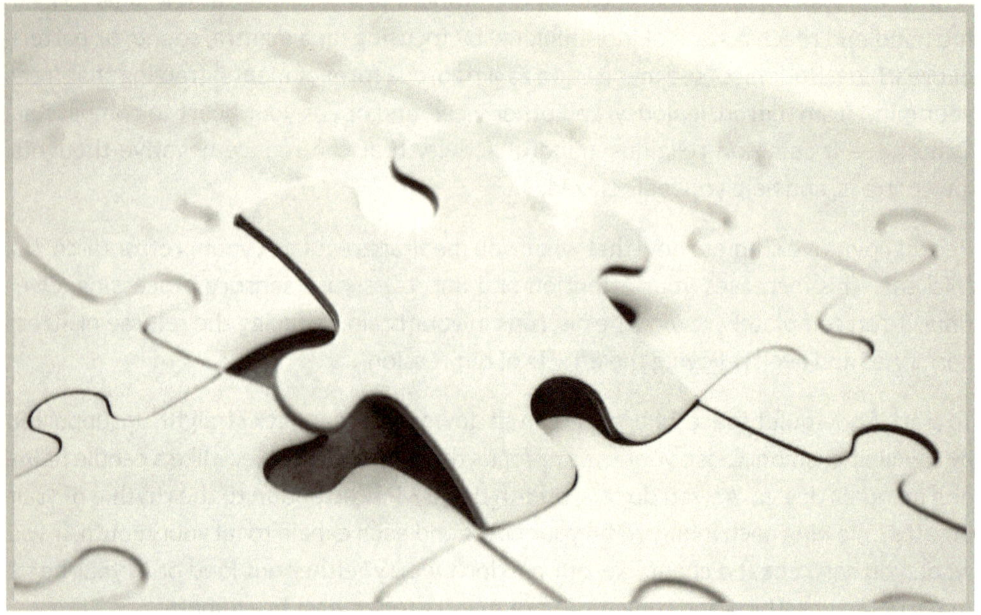

Figure 11: Puzzles improve your concentration, problem-solving skills, and spatial memory (Alexas_Fotos, 2018).

Although they are less aesthetically pleasing, sudoku, kakuro and other number puzzles improve concentration and deductive reasoning skills. Additionally, word puzzles like crosswords and anagrams test your linguistic skills, helping you to learn new words and strengthen your verbal memory.

Why not give all three types of puzzles a go and see where it takes you? They could give you that extra mental boost you need for tomorrow's brain training exercise.

Mapping

As we've seen with the Journey Method and Memory Palace Method from Chapter 4, location is a key feature of memory training, because it provides one of the easiest methods of association.

Yet, it's not just mnemonic techniques that improve your spatial memory. Looking at and creating maps is an effective way to strengthen your knowledge of different locations in relation to each other.

Studies show that reading maps causes your hippocampus to grow, which heightens your spatial awareness. It's also a useful skill that can improve your muscle memory, allowing your feet to automatically direct you to your frequent destinations by visualizing this map in your mind.

Want to improve your memory even further? Try creating your own maps. These could be of present-day locations you're familiar with, historically or geographically distant locations you'd like to learn more about, or imagined locations, like a fictional town from your favorite book or a fantasy world from your favorite video game. By concentrating on plotting each location, sketching the environment, and creating a legend, you'll exercise different parts of your brain. Who knows? You may even discover a new favorite hobby.

Video Games

This one may seem surprising. Yet, recent studies show that playing video games may actually improve your short-term memory. Gamers report many benefits off-screen, including improved reaction times, greater hand dexterity, and heightened spatial awareness. Some studies also suggest that playing video games may increase your attention span, as long as you're gaming in moderation.

Moderation is the key word here. If you're spending most of your day indoors, hunched over a chair playing Xbox, then you're not likely getting the proper sensory stimulation and blood flow that your brain needs in order to function at its best. In Chapter 9, we'll discuss some of these healthy habits that will help you take your memory training even further.

CHAPTER - 08

Healthy Habits

Your memory training doesn't have to end with learning the Major System or starting a dream journal. There are plenty of everyday habits you can adopt to take your memory power to the next level, while nurturing both your mind and your body.

In this chapter, you'll learn how to take care of your brain by paying attention to how you stand, what kind of foods you eat, how often you go outdoors, how often you exercise, how much sleep you get, which essential oils you use, and how much alcohol and drugs you consume. Adopting healthy habits to take care of your overall health will ensure that your brain training works to its maximum extent.

Posture

Posture may seem like a strange consideration, but it's an often overlooked factor of brain health. When you sit or stand up straight, your windpipe and blood vessels are unrestricted (Buzan & Harrison, 2010). This means that your brain will benefit from the maximum flow of oxygen and blood, improving your focus and memory.

Maintaining an upright posture at a table also keeps your eyes at the perfect height to your workbook, tablet, or laptop screen. This maximizes your central and peripheral vision, allowing you to take in more information at once and thus work more quickly and efficiently.

If you're used to slouching, correcting your posture may seem unnatural at first. But it's important to make a conscious effort to suck in your stomach, puff out your chest, relax your shoulders, bend your knees slightly, and keep your feet flat on the floor. Once you get used to it, your muscle memory will take over and you'll be slouch-free. Your brain—and your back—will thank you for it.

Diet

Brains are hungry organs, consuming up to 20% of your body's total energy (Harrison & Hobbs, 2010; O'Brien, 2016; Success Sculpting Coach, 2005). Because of this, it's important to keep yourself well-nourished with food that's high in brain-boosting nutrients, like carbohydrates, protein, fatty acids, vitamins, and minerals.

Carbohydrates are your body's basic source of energy. Your stomach and small intestine break down complex carbs into simple sugars, which are transported to your brain to nourish your neurons. Corn, beets, beans, legumes, whole grains, and nuts are all rich in carbs as well as *protein*. Proteins are chains of amino acids, which are essential for basic brain functions, like repairing damaged neurons, producing hormones, and regulating stress.

Aside from high-carb and high-protein meals, the best brain food also contains high levels of *omega-3s*. These *fatty acids* are responsible for building stronger connections between neurons. You can get these primarily from oily fish like salmon and mackerel, as well as from eggs, avocados, seaweed, and olive oil. Eggs also have *choline*, an amino acid-type nutrient that has been linked to improved memory. Additionally, avocados—along with blueberries, kale, oats, and green tea—are rich in *antioxidants*. Antioxidants maintain healthy neurons by destroying harmful molecules called "free radicals."

You can find antioxidants in any food with high amounts of *Vitamins A, C,* and *E*, which all play important roles in maintaining brain health. Vitamin A, found in liver, carrots, sweet potatoes, and butter, is responsible for improving your vision, which aids your visual memory. Nuts, like almonds, are an excellent source of dementia-fighting Vitamin E, as are hazelnuts and cashews. Finally, immune system-boosting Vitamin C can be found in citrus fruits, berries, and leafy greens.

B and *D* Vitamins are also important for brain health. Vitamin B6 converts blood sugar to glucose to supply your brain with nutrients. You can get this from cereals, meat, bananas, and chickpeas. Folic acid is another B vitamin that helps with depression. It can be found in liver, legumes, leafy greens and nuts. Finally, Vitamin D, which is found in oily fish, egg yolks, and mushrooms, helps you absorb minerals like magnesium and phosphate, which make up the DNA and RNA in neurons and other cells.

Other important memory-friendly nutritional supplements include zinc, another antioxidant, and Ginkgo Biloba, a natural medicine from maidenhair trees.

Best of all, dark chocolate has proven to hold numerous health benefits. It has three times as many antioxidants as green tea and contains a high level of magnesium. One study showed that patients who were given a 1.6 oz piece of dark chocolate everyday experienced less chronic fatigue and better alertness than those who weren't.

Yet, although it is low in sugar and artificial sweeteners, dark chocolate also contains caffeine. Caffeine and sweeteners may give you a short-term energy boost, but they may actually be detrimental to your long-term memory, making you feel more tired and less focused. So, instead of reaching for a mid-day coffee, try grabbing a handful of nuts and fruit smoothie instead. You'll be surprised by a more powerful—and longer lasting—energy boost.

Fresh Air

Working or studying full-time may mean that you spend most of your time indoors, especially if you live in a rainy or snowy climate. Yet, it is important to get some fresh outdoor air as often as you can. There are two main reasons for this (Success Sculpting Coach, 2005).

Firstly, fresh air increases the oxygen supply to your brain. This enables you to think clearer and faster, boosting your memory in the process.

Secondly, going outside provides more mental stimulation than sitting indoors. Regularly introducing your senses to new sights, sounds, and smells raises your energy level, improves your focus, and helps you become less forgetful.

Even if you can't physically go outdoors, you can still benefit from sitting by an open window, where you can recharge your oxygen supply and look for interesting sights and sounds in between chapters or emails.

Exercise

Regular exercise is an essential habit for maintaining brain health (Harrison & Hobbs, 2010). When you raise your heart rate, you increase the blood flow to your prefrontal cortex and other memory-associated areas of your brain. Studies show that seniors who regularly exercise have better memories and attention spans than those who don't. Even for healthy young adults, most doctors recommend daily exercise consisting of either half an hour of moderate-intensity activities, short bursts of high-intensity activities, or long periods of low-intensity activities.

Aerobic exercises are designed to keep your heart rate up and increase your oxygen levels. These can include any activity that keeps you constantly moving for 15 minutes or longer, like walking, dancing, cycling, kickboxing, swimming, cross-country skiing, or playing basketball. With so many aerobic options to choose from, you'll be sure to find one that you enjoy.

Meditation-based exercises like yoga, tai chi, and qigong are also important to practice on a regular basis. As we discussed in Chapter 7, meditation has been proven to clear your mind, reduce stress, and improve sleep, all of which improve your brain health. Even if you're not into child's pose or dancing crane, you can still incorporate meditation into your other exercise. For example, you could wind down from a spin class or soccer game with at least ten minutes of light stretching and deep breathing. Doing this will refocus your mind and maximize the benefits of your higher-intensity exercise.

Other useful exercises are ones that improve your hand-eye and eye-foot coordination, like tennis, hacky sack, juggling, dance, and tai chi. These carefully thought out movements not only take your mind off daily stresses by focusing on the task at hand, they also boost your brainpower by strengthening your cerebellum, which, as we've discussed previously, plays an important role in certain aspects of memory (Amen, 2017).

Whatever exercises you decide to participate in, it's essential that you choose something that you enjoy. A study on lab mice found that even older ones who ran voluntarily on their treadmills showed neurogenesis and increased learning (Begley, 2008). Yet, those who were forced to run did not. It may take a while, but if you try out as many activities as you can, you'll be sure to find the right aerobic, meditation, and coordination exercises to help keep your brain healthy.

Sleep

Getting a good night's sleep is something so many of us lack (Figure 12). But it's one of the most essential factors to maintaining a healthy memory. After all, just like our electronic devices, our brains need to recharge when we run out of energy, so that they can properly function once they wake up.

Figure 12: Lack of sleep is one of the key factors in forgetfulness and memory loss (Gorn, 2017).

When you sleep, your body releases hormones to repair damaged brain tissue (Harrison

& Hobbs, 2010). It is also during sleep that your brain reviews what you've experienced during the day and transfers important information from your working memory into your long-term memory. Lack of sleep leads to stress, which reduces neurogenesis. Over time, this can create lasting damage on your memories.

Some people can function on five hours of sleep per night, others need nine. Once you've found which works better for you, you'll be able to plan a schedule to maximize your necessary sleep times. It may take a while to get used to, but try to keep your body on a regular schedule, even on weekends. This will make it easier to get in the habit of sleeping for five to nine hours every night.

Naps can also be a great way to give yourself an energy boost during the day. Some research shows that even a six-minute nap can improve your memory. But if you sleep for more than 20 minutes, you may wake up more drowsy than when you laid down. This is because our REM (rapid eye movement) or deep-sleep cycle kicks in around this point. Waking up in the middle of your cycle can make you feel disoriented and irritable. Therefore, if you need to nap for more than 20 minutes, it's best to wake up at the end of your cycle, around the one-and-a-half hour mark.

If you have trouble going to sleep at night, try avoiding stimulants like caffeine and alcohol and using heavy curtains, sleep masks, and other tools to eliminate light and noise. You should eat no less than three hours before bedtime, giving your body time to digest any sugars that might keep you up. They also recommend performing relaxing pre-bedtime rituals, like taking a warm bath, listening to light music, or reading a book. Doing this will help calm your mind, inviting sleep to take over and rejuvenate your brain.

Aromatherapy

Memories associated with smell are often more intense than memories associated with the other senses. Harrison & Hobbs (2010) argue that because of its association with the rhinal cortex, smell has more of an emotional basis than sight or hearing. This is why we are often transported back to certain places or reminded of certain people when we smell things that remind us of them.

Based on this connection, many researchers are interested in how certain herbs and oils can trigger memory. For example, Lopresti (2017) found that both younger and older adults who were exposed to sage oil reported faster recall of information than those who were not. Yet, it is important to be careful when burning or ingesting sage. Some species contain large amounts of a toxic compound called thujone, which can cause psychotic effects. To keep yourself safe, always talk to your doctor before trying natural medicine and check the thujone levels before you buy any sage oil.

Unfortunately, there is no large-scale body of evidence to suggest that essential oils like sage can be used to treat dementia or to help people remember specific information. Still, because of its calming effects and evocative smell, it may still play a small-scale role in improving everyday memory.

Substance Intake

So far, we've focused on the things to do in order to improve memory. Yet there are also things that should be avoided. More specifically, this includes ingesting large and frequent quantities of mind-altering substances.

Alcohol is a toxin that is notorious for destroying brain cells (Amen, 2017; Success Sculpting Coach, 2005). After all, this is why many people wake up after a heavy night of drinking unable to remember what happened to them the night before. Your brain is constantly creating new neurons. Yet, neurons are destroyed by alcohol consumption more quickly than they can be made, which causes your brain to shrink, resulting in memory loss. Frequent alcohol consumption also leads to depression, which alters your brain chemistry, making it more difficult to form strong, long-term memories.

Marijuana is another toxin with a dangerous effect on your brain (Ilan, et al., 2004). It interferes with the receptors in your prefrontal cortex and hippocampus, making it more difficult to convert short-term memories. This is why frequent marijuana use has been linked to diminished working memory and episodic memory.

By limiting your alcohol and drug intake, maintaining an upright posture, getting lots of fresh outdoor air, eating food with brain-rich nutrients, getting a proper amount of sleep, experimenting with low-thujone sage oil, and engaging in frequent aerobic, meditation-based, and coordination-based exercises, you can rest assured that your healthy habits will help cement your memory training even further. It may take a few weeks to get into these healthy habits. Yet, your brain and body will thank you in the long run.

CHAPTER - 09

Things to Keep in Mind

By this point, you've probably been working on your memory training for a while. You've completed the exercises at the end of Chapters 3 to 6. You've done some kakuro puzzles, taken a quick walk outside, and maybe even stopped at the health food store for some ginkgo biloba.

As you progress in your memory training, there may be times where you start to feel frustrated. Maybe you've mastered the first three items on your list with your Dominic Code, but Number 4 Bobby Orr still flies off into some misty, unknown location. Maybe you're still forgetting Angie's, Ugo's, and Gurinder's names when you see them at meetings. Maybe it's been four days and you still can't remember where you left your garage keys.

All of this is perfectly normal. No marathon runner ever managed 26 miles the first time they laced up their running shoes. They had to train for months or even years to reach that milestone. The same goes for brain training too. It takes a lot of time and effort to master the mnemonic techniques we've discussed in this book. But the payoff is well worth it.

Here are some important things to keep in mind while continuing your memory training. Reminding yourself of these facts whenever you're feeling down will renew your focus, boost your confidence, and propel your memory to new levels.

You Can Learn Anything at Any Age and Any Level of Education

As we discussed in Chapter 1, our brains are much more flexible than experts once thought (Buzan, 2006; Harrison & Hobbs, 2010). We are constantly growing new neurons and forming new synaptic connections between existing neurons. Even in older adults, the human brain has an apparently limitless capacity, with our brain size and weight staying constant until the age of 90. Some studies show our memories may even improve as we get older, as we form more and more connections in our brains.

What does this mean for you? It means that you can learn as much as you want, any time that you want, at any age.

There's no reason why a 60-year-old cannot calculate days of the week with any more difficulty than a 16-year-old, except that a 16-year-old high school student may have more energy and focus to invest in their brain training compared to a 60-year-old grandparent with a full-time job and weekend babysitting responsibilities. Yet, as long as you dedicate a few minutes every day to brain training, you'll be surprised that even in your senior years, you can take your memory power to brand new levels.

The best part is, you don't even need a university degree to master mnemonic techniques. Dominic O'Brien dropped out of school at age sixteen after struggling to master his school subjects (2016). Yet, by taking the time to improve his memory skills, he eventually went on to win eight world championships.

In short, no one is born with a good memory. But by dedicating yourself to brain training, you can boost your intelligence, improve your focus, and defy any limitations of your age or educational level.

Brains Are Not Hard Drives

Again, as we discussed in Chapter 1, organic memory is a very different process from computer memory. Computer memory is more like a high-tech filing system, where we can add whatever information we want and randomly extract the file whenever we need it (Figure 13; Harrison & Hobbs, 2010). Yet, our brains are not hard drives. We may have some difficulty recalling our memories from time to time, especially when we're distracted by other things. And unless we make the necessary associations, we may not be able to convert our working memories into long-term memories.

Figure 13: Unlike floppy disks and other forms of electronic memory, our brains have unlimited storage space—and never become obsolete (Jacob, 2018).

However, there is some good news. Unlike computers, our minds have unlimited 'terabytes' of storage space. This means that the information we hold in our brains far exceeds the available space in any laptop on earth. Furthermore, our long-term memories cannot be 'deleted.' We may forget them temporarily, but they are always there in some part of our brain. We simply need to forge the right connections in order to recall them.

So, don't beat yourself up if you can't remember the sixth item on your grocery list or flubbed the final answer to your anthropology exam. As long as you keep practicing your mnemonic techniques and perfecting your study habits, recalling this type of information will soon become second nature.

All It Takes Is Fifteen Minutes

You're probably a busy person. After spending six hours in a lecture hall or eight hours in a cubicle, then hitting the gym, making dinner, doing the load of laundry you've been putting off for three days, and trying to get to bed at a decent hour, brain training may be the last thing you want to think about.

Yet, to really start seeing results, it's best to do at least some form of memory training for fifteen minutes a day. If you can do more, all the better. But fifteen minutes is enough time to start forming those new synaptic connections.

To make things easier, try completing your fifteen minutes at the same time every day, preferably close to a daily activity that you also do at a regular time. For example, it's a lot easier to remember your brain training schedule if you're always doing it after you eat a meal or before you go to bed. It's also best to complete your training during the time of day when you feel the most relaxed and alert. If you're a morning person, you might want to schedule your brain training between the time you eat breakfast and go to school or work. If you're an afternoon person, you might want to schedule it during your lunch break. Or, if you're an evening person, you might want to schedule it half an hour or so before you go to bed. Try a few different time slots at the beginning and see what works best for you.

Still finding it hard to make the time? Why not incorporate some brain training throughout your day? Do a sudoku puzzle while you eat breakfast. Create a short rhyme that includes all the stationary items on your desk. Peg all the clothes you need to wash in your Memory Palace. Small activities like this can bring you the same benefits as sitting down at your desk and consciously working through exercises. Plus, the more you connect mnemonic techniques to tasks you do every day, the more likely you'll be able to remember them and benefit from them.

Breaks Are Important

Have you been staring at your list of memory words for minutes on end, unable to come up with a memorable image for the number 7 or someone you know with the initials S.G? Take a break. Watch a YouTube video, listen to a song, or do a series of squats and jumping jacks. Do whatever helps you relax and recharge. If you try to force your memory, you'll only end up tiring yourself out. Yet, by taking frequent breaks, you'll be able to come back to whatever you're working on feeling refreshed and focused.

Studies also show that we tend to remember the most information from the beginning and end of our learning periods (Buzan & Harrison, 2010). Taking frequent two- to ten-minute breaks creates more peak beginnings and ends, thus maximizing your likelihood of retaining information. Especially when starting your brain training, you'll probably find it easier to split your fifteen minutes into one ten-minute and one five-minute session. As you're able to successfully memorize more and more things, you can gradually increase your learning sessions to fifteen, thirty, or even sixty minute sessions. Just be patient with yourself and stop as soon as your mind starts to wander.

Still feeling guilty about going for a quick snack in the middle of rehearsing for your presentation or memorizing your number-shapes? Don't be. According to Buzan (2006), your brain still processes the information you're trying to learn, even when you take breaks. When you let your mind run loose and focus on other things, you may even recall information that you thought you'd forgotten, like another feature of your proposed video-sharing app or the cliff face you drew for the number 7. This technique is especially important when Reliving the Immediate Relevant Past, as we discussed in Chapter 5.

Of course, taking breaks doesn't mean that you should procrastinate, extending your breaks to hours on end. Stick as closely as you can to your ten-minute study intervals, with no more than ten minutes in between. By doing so, you'll retain all the benefits of what you've learned without tiring yourself out in the process.

No Memory Is Perfect

You did your best. You set aside a few minutes after breakfast each day to work on your mnemonic systems and mind mapping skills, sitting up straight in a quiet room with no distractions. You split each session with a ten-minute meditation. After each session, you went for a run, using your map of the neighborhood to check out new streets you'd never been to before. You returned home after each run and ate a spinach salad with smoked salmon, walnuts, and olive oil dressing. You ended each day by burning a sage incense stick and settling in for a 9-hour sleep. You did everything you're supposed to do for two weeks. Yet, you still flubbed that important presentation at work. Then forgot where you left your cell phone. So, what now?

The truth is, no memory is perfect. We all make mistakes from time to time, even when we've been brain training for months or even years. You can use your mistakes as an excuse to give up. You can go back to your old habits of reading from notes at your podium and perpetually asking your housemates if they've seen your phone lying around.

Or you could keep going. You could remind yourself of all the amazing things you've accomplished so far, even if it's something small like remembering your neighbor's birthday or answering that one question that no one else knew at your family game night. You could see your current mistakes as learning opportunities. You could use them as an incentive to spur you onward, putting even more effort into your brain training and receiving even greater mental rewards.

The choice is yours. Yet, if you do decide not to give up and to continually work on your memory, you'll start to see improvements, bit by bit. Over time, your wins will outnumber your mistakes and you'll amaze yourself by how limitless your memory truly is.

Conclusion

Congratulations! You've just finished your introduction to memory training. Hopefully, this book has convinced you that with the right tools at your disposal, you can unlock your full potential as a memory whiz.

By now, you've learned how to:

> Identify the parts of your brain that are associated with different types of memory
> Distinguish the different types of intelligences and apply them to your memory-training plan
> Create and use mnemonic devices, systems, methods, and task-specific techniques to remember anything from shopping lists to important numbers to foreign language words to forgotten objects around your house
> Improve your reading, writing, studying, and reviewing skills
> Participate in fun hobbies that also boost your memory potential
> Adopt healthy eating, sitting, exercising, and sleeping habits to improve your memory
> And finally, give yourself that extra vote of confidence whenever you feel frustrated and consider giving up

Memories don't improve overnight. It takes a lot of time, energy, and effort to master the techniques discussed in this book. Even after breezing through these techniques, you may be a long piece away from beating the records of Dominic O'Brien, Ben Pridmore, Dr. Yip Swe Chooi, or Boris Nikolai Konrad.

Yet, with the right amount of practice, you might someday be the next world champion, or at least your local pub quiz champion. Or maybe you'll just be the only person in your house that knows what *antediluvian* means and remembers exactly where they left their car keys. Any accomplishment, no matter how small, is a reason to celebrate.

So, give yourself a pat on the back and a big round of applause. Hoot and holler loud enough to wake the neighbors. You deserve it.

Then, grab a notebook, prop your tablet or ereader against something sturdy, and put all that hard work to good use by applying the mnemonic techniques you've learned to learn the following:

A shopping list: **chips, roses, earbuds, soy sauce, nail polish, toy car**

Four world capitals: **Suva** (Fiji), **Yerevan** (Armenia), **Kingston** (Jamaica), **Ankara** (Turkey)

The seven modes of western music: **Ionian, Dorian, Phrygian, Lydian, Mixoldyian, Aeolian, Locrian**

The five most-populated African countries (as of 2019): **Nigeria**, **Ethiopia**, **Egypt**, **Democratic Republic of Congo**, **Tanzania**

The proper spellings of: **embarrassed, recommend, independent, dilemma**

The Dutch-to-English translations of: **koning** (king), **aardappel** (potato), **gezellig** (cozy/sociable), **boos** (angry), **vallen** (to fall), **kijken** (to watch)

This order of playing cards: **ace of spades**, **king of clubs**, **jack of diamonds**, **four of diamonds**, **eight of hearts**

The year Genghis Khan came to power: **1206**

The day of the week that Martin Luther King Jr was born: **January 15th, 1929**

The speed of light: **299,792,458 m/s**

This pin number: **5932**

This binary code: **001111100010**

That's it. You've mastered all of these exercises in this book. So, what happens next?

Luckily, there's plenty of other books, as well as websites, apps, videos, and podcasts, to help you out as you continue to work hard each day to improve your memory.

Additional Resources

Ready for more memory training tips, tricks, and exercises? Here's a short list to get started:

Books

Brain Training: Boost Memory, Maximize Mental Agility, & Awaken Your Inner Genius by James Harrison and Mike Hobbs – a book containing a variety of brain-training activities, where you can test the Journey Method and Peg System, create mind maps, and solve puzzles.

How to Develop a Brilliant Memory Week by Week by Dominic O'Brien – a book full of memory-boosting exercises, like creating acronyms, remembering binary numbers, and developing your own Dominic code.

Use Your Memory by Tony Buzan – this book forms the basis of the mnemonic systems and methods we discussed in Chapters 4 and 5. There's also lots of practice exercises to test your knowledge of the Link System, the Roman Room Method (Memory Palace Method), and the Social Etiquette Method, among others.

Websites

AcademicTips.org – a great resource written by college educators for learning more about mnemonic systems. It also includes tips for studying, writing essays, and managing stress.

Arkadium – a website full of free jigsaw, number, and word puzzles.

Coggle – an online mind-mapping tool, where you can create three free mind maps per month.

Lumosity – an online brain-training program based on fun mini-games developed by cognitive scientists. You can access three games per day on the free version, as well as personal stats to track your progress. Also available as an app on iOS and Android.

Apps

Elevate – a brain-training app with a serious feel and text-based approach. You can complete three mini-games per day in the free version and also compare your progress to others in your age group. Available on iOS and Android.

Fit Brains – a brain-training app with additional games that focus on emotional intelligence. Available on iOS and Android.

Mindly – a virtual mind-map creator, free for maps with less than 200 elements. Available on MacOS, iOS, and Android.

Peak – a brain-training app developed with help from leading scientists. It also has activities tailored for all ages. Available on iOS and Android.

YouTube Channels

Anthony Metivier – focusing on the Memory Palace method, memory expert Anthony Metivier teaches you how to use mnemonic techniques to get rid of "senior moments," remember passwords, and even memorize textbooks.

Bright Side – includes short videos about tips, tricks, and exercises to improve your memory.

TEDx Talks – includes talks from memory champions and study experts like Boris Nikolai Konrad, Ricardo Lieuw On, and Krishan Chahal.

Podcasts

Anthony Metivier's Magnetic Memory Method Podcast – Anthony Metivier takes you through effective ways to maximize your foreign language vocabulary. Available on Google Podcasts, iTunes, and Stitcher.

Master of Memory – educator Timothy Moser covers useful mnemonic techniques for a variety of topics, from learning languages to navigating memory palaces to even memorizing books. Available on iTunes and Stitcher, and at masterofmemory.com

The SuperHuman Academy Podcast – learning expert Jonathan Levi invites special guests each week to cover topics like beating procrastination, improving your sleep, and maximizing your concentration. Available on Google Podcasts, iTunes, Overcast, Spotify, and Stitcher, and at superhumanacademy.com

References

- Adrian. (2018). *Board chalk business*. In *Pixabay*. https://pixabay.com/photos/board-chalk-business-job-work-3695073/

- Alexas_Fotos. (2018). Puzzle last part joining together. In *Pixabay*. https://pixabay.com/photos/puzzle-last-part-joining-together-3223941/

- Altmann, G. (2017). Man old view question. In *Pixabay*. https://pixabay.com/photos/man-old-view-question-mark-2546107/

- Altmann, G. (2019). Knowledge spark flash. In *Pixabay*. https://pixabay.com/photos/knowledge-spark-flash-hand-think-3914811/

- Amen, D. G. (2018). *Memory rescue: Supercharge your brain, reverse memory loss, and remember what matters most.* Tyndale Momentum. https://www.amazon.com/Memory-Rescue-Supercharge-Reverse-Remember-ebook/dp/B06XKCL7NR

- Assmann, A. (2008). Canon and archive. In A. Erll & A. Nünning (Eds.), *Cultural Memory Studies: An International and Interdisciplinary Handbook* (pp. 97–108). Walter De Gruyter. https://files.cercomp.ufg.br/weby/up/113/o/astrid_erll__ansgar_nünning_(eds.)_-_cultural_memory_studies._an_international_and_interdisciplinary_handbook.pdf?1337708248#page=397

- Begley, S. (2008). *Train your mind, change your brain : how a new science reveals our extraordinary potential to transform ourselves.* Ballantine Books. https://www.pdfdrive.com/train-your-mind-change-your-brain-how-a-new-science-reveals-our-extraordinary-potential-to-transform-ourselves-d157740836.html

- Buissine, S. (2016). Elephant trunk big. In *Pixabay*. https://pixabay.com/photos/elephant-trunk-big-african-1526709/

- Buzan, T. (2006). *Use your memory.* BBC Active. https://www.pdfdrive.com/tony-buzan-use-your-memory-mega-brain-mind-memory-d16144340.html

- Buzan, T., & Harrison, J. (2010). *The Buzan study skills handbook.* BBC Active. https://www.pdfdrive.com/buzan-study-skills-handbook-the-shortcut-to-success-in-your-studies-with-mind-mapping-speed-reading-and-winning-memory-techniques-mind-set-d156806686.html

- Chancellor, B., Duncan, A., & Chatterjee, A. (2014). Art therapy for Alzheimer's Disease and other dementias. *Journal of Alzheimer's Disease, 39*, 1–11. https://doi.org/https://doi.org/10.3233/jad-131295

- Consino, A. (2008). Memory and the history of mentalities. In A. Erll & A. Nünning (Eds.), *Cultural Memory Studies: An International and Interdisciplinary Handbook* (pp. 77–84). Walter De Gruyter. https://files.cercomp.ufg.br/weby/up/113/o/astrid_erll__ansgar_nünning_(eds.)_-_cultural_memory_studies._an_international_and_interdisciplinary_handbook.pdf?1337708248#page=397

- Cytonn Photography. (2018). Two people shaking hands. In *Unsplash*. https://unsplash.com/photos/n95VMLxqM2I

- Davis, G. M., & Fan, W. (2016). English vocabulary acquisition through songs in Chinese kindergarten students. *Chinese Journal of Applied Linguistics, 39*(1), 59–71. https://doi.org/10.1515/cjal-2016-0004

- The Derek Bok Center for Teaching and Learning. (2011). *How memory works*. Harvard.Edu. https://bokcenter.harvard.edu/how-memory-works

- G, N. (2015). First Nation headdress feather. In *Pixabay*. https://pixabay.com/photos/first-nation-headdress-feather-908604/

- Gardner, H., & Hatch, T. (1989). Multiple intelligences go to school: Educational implications of the theory of multiple intelligences. *Educational Researcher, 18*(8), 4–10. https://doi.org/10.2307/1176460

- Gorn, A. (2017). Woman covering her face with blanket. In *Unsplash*. https://unsplash.com/photos/smuS_jUZa9I

- Harrison, J., & Hobbs, M. (2010). *Brain Training: Boost Memory, Maximize Mental Agility, & Awaken Your Inner Genius*. DK. https://www.pdfdrive.com/brain-training-boost-memory-maximize-mental-agility-awaken-your-inner-genius-d162242543.html

- Higbee, K. L. (2001). Mnemonics, psychology of. *International Encyclopedia of the Social & Behavioral Sciences*, 9915–9918. https://doi.org/10.1016/b0-08-043076-7/01517-5

- Ilan, A. B., Smith, M. E., & Gevins, A. (2004). Effects of marijuana on neurophysiological signals of working and episodic memory. *Psychopharmacology, 176*(2), 214–222. https://doi.org/10.1007/s00213-004-1868-9

- Jacob, F., 2018. Red and white floppy disk on white. In *Unsplash*. https://unsplash.com/photos/tOSlmanfFcg

- Karabulut, M. (2019). Street Islamic girl. In *Pixabay* https://pixabay.com/photos/street-islamic-girl-old-walk-4203906/

- Levitin, D. J., & Cook, P. R. (1996). Memory for musical tempo: Additional evidence that auditory memory is absolute. *Perception & Psychophysics, 58*(6), 927–935. https://doi.org/10.3758/bf03205494

- Lopresti, A. L. (2016). Salvia (sage): A review of its potential cognitive-enhancing and protective effects. *Drugs in R&D, 17*(1), 53–64. https://doi.org/10.1007/s40268-016-0157-5

- Memory. (n.d.). In *Merriam-Webster*. Retrieved May 23, 2020, from https://www.merriam-webster.com/dictionary/memory

- *Memory techniques - learning foreign languages*. (n.d.). AcademicTips.org. https://www.academictips.org/memory/forlangu.html

- Nielsen, J. A., Zielinski, B. A., Ferguson, M. A., Lainhart, J. E., & Anderson, J. S. (2013). An Evaluation of the Left-Brain vs. Right-Brain Hypothesis with Resting State Functional Connectivity Magnetic Resonance Imaging. *PLoS ONE, 8*(8), e71275. https://doi.org/10.1371/journal.pone.0071275

- Nyberg, L., Sandblom, J., Jones, S., Neely, A. S., Petersson, K. M., Ingvar, M., & Backman, L. (2003). Neural correlates of training-related memory improvement in adulthood and aging. *Proceedings of the National Academy of Sciences, 100*(23), 13728–13733. https://doi.org/10.1073/pnas.1735487100

- O'Brien, D. (2016). *How to develop a brilliant memory week by week: 52 proven ways to enhance your memory skills*. https://www.pdfdrive.com/how-to-develop-a-brilliant-memory-week-by-week-52-proven-ways-to-enhance-your-memory-skills-e158322599.html

- Ranya. (2015). Ancient Greek temple of. In *Pixabay*. https://pixabay.com/photos/ancient-greek-temple-590682/

- Smoker, T. J., Murphy, C. E., & Rockwell, A. K. (2009). Comparing memory for handwriting versus typing. *Proceedings of the Human Factors and Ergonomics Society Annual Meeting, 53*(22), 1744–1747. https://doi.org/10.1177/154193120905302218

- Success Sculpting Coach. (2005). *How to improve memory: The ultimate mind power manual*. Success Sculpting Inc. https://www.pdfdrive.com/how-to-improve-memory-the-ultimate-mind-power-manual-the-best-brain-exercises-to-improve-your-memory-and-master-your-mind-power-e194501770.html

- TEDx Talks. (2016). The mind and methods of a memory champion | Boris Nikolai Konrad | TEDxStrijp [YouTube Video]. In *YouTube*. https://www.youtube.com/watch?v=t76N00urDlU&feature=youtu.be&t=6m34s

- Weirmeijer, R. (2019). Human brain toy photo. In *Unsplash*. https://unsplash.com/photos/lHfOpAzzjHM

- Wimber, M., Alink, A., Charest, I., Kriegeskorte, N., & Anderson, M. C. (2015). Retrieval induces adaptive forgetting of competing memories via cortical pattern suppression. *Nature Neuroscience, 18*(4), 582–589. https://doi.org/10.1038/nn.3973

- Wong, W. (2017). Selective focus photography of people. In *Unsplash*. https://unsplash.com/photos/ooclshMwAQk